THE PRESOCRATICS

THE
PRESOCRATICS

Edward Hussey

Published in the U.K. by
Gerald Duckworth & Co. Ltd.
London

Published in North America by
Hackett Publishing Company, Inc.
Indianapolis/Cambridge

First published in 1972 by
Gerald Duckworth & Co. Ltd.

Reissued in 1995 by
Bristol Classical Press
an imprint of
Gerald Duckworth & Co. Ltd.
The Old Piano Factory
48 Hoxton Square, London N1 6PB

and by

Hackett Publishing Company, Inc.
P.O. Box 44937
Indianapolis, Indiana 46244-0937

U.K. Edition: U.S. Edition:
ISBN 1-85399-485-5   ISBN 0-87220-276-3 (pbk.)
A CIP catalogue record for   ISBN 0-87220-277-1
this book is available from
the British Library   LC 95-80650

The paper used in this publication meets the minimum
requirements of American National Standard for Information
Sciences—Permanence of Paper for Printed Library
Materials, ANSI Z39.48-1984.
∞
Printed in the United States of America

Contents

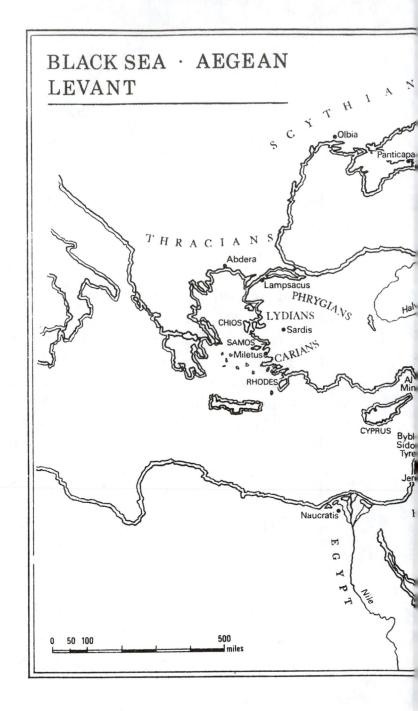

BLACK SEA · AEGEAN
LEVANT

SCYTHIANS

Olbia

Panticapa

THRACIANS

Abdera

Lampsacus

PHRYGIANS

Halv

CHIOS

LYDIANS

Sardis

SAMOS

Miletus

CARIANS

RHODES

A
Min

CYPRUS

Byb
Sido
Tyre

Jer

Naucratis

EGYPT

Nile

H

0 50 100   500
                             miles

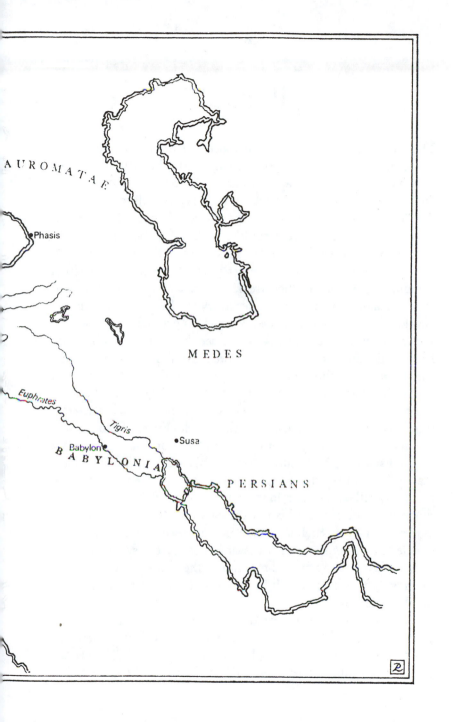

AUROMATAE

•Phasis

MEDES

Euphrates

Tigris

Babylon• •Susa

BABYLONIA

PERSIANS

Preface

The aim of this book is to introduce the reader, without presupposing any knowledge of Greek, to the history of ancient Greek thought between approximately 600 and 400 B.C. Most of the individual thinkers with whom it deals are traditionally given the description 'Presocratic philosophers'—hence the title; but the book does not entirely confine itself to the activities of the people so described. In order to make a comprehensible picture, it is necessary to set them against a background of intellectual stimulus from outside the Greek world, and of economic and social change inside it; it is necessary to keep an eye on the development of particular sciences such as geometry, astronomy and medicine; and it is necessary to trace the connections between Presocratic innovations and the more general outburst of mental energy in the 'sophistic' period at the end of the fifth century. In a book of this length, many parts of the picture can be only sketched; I have given more elaborate treatment to what seemed to me to be more significant for the development of philosophy and science. The scarcity of direct evidence on many important questions is a severe limitation on any book of this kind. In some places, I have thought it right to give space to speculations supported by little or nothing in the way of direct evidence. In others, the interpretation offered is not the only one consistent with such evidence as there is; but I have not exposed the reader to the detailed controversies that necessarily occupy the specialists, and I have often not so much as mentioned the existence of divergent opinions, though these will be found in plenty in the books and articles listed in the Notes.

The references incorporated in the text are to the more important of the ancient sources cited or alluded to. These references are given on the system explained in the Notes. A short account of the ancient sources will be found in Chapter Eight.

CHAPTER ONE

Introduction

'PRESOCRATIC' is a word coined in order to make it possible to group together certain Greek thinkers who lived not later than the time of Socrates and were not decisively influenced by him. What else this group had in common is not immediately obvious. They are sometimes called 'the first philosophers' or 'the first scientists', but these descriptions are misleading. 'Science' and 'philosophy', as activities distinguishable one from another and from other ways of thinking about the world, came into existence only at the end of the Presocratic period. What gives the group of Presocratics such unity as it possesses is rather that all these men were involved in the movement of thought which led to the separation of science and philosophy from one another and from other ways of thinking.

This movement of thought has no definite beginning or end, but there are two convenient discontinuities which make 'Presocratic' a not too artificial classification. The later discontinuity is the revolution in thought associated with Socrates and his disciples; the earlier one, because of the lack of information, is more mysterious and less easily described. At some time in the first half of the sixth century,* in the Greek city of Miletus in Asia Minor, there were men who began to reason about the universe in a way which was hitherto unknown in Greece, and in all probability was influenced by ideas derived from the older civilisations of the Near East. The thinkers of Miletus are the subject of the next chapter; something must be said now about the world into which they were born.

*

* All dates in this book are B.C. unless expressly stated to be A.D.

The collapse of Mycenean civilisation, and the subsequent troubles of the early Iron Age, brought a period of material and cultural impoverishment in Greece. Early in this 'Dark Age', perhaps around 1000, the eastern seaboard of Asia Minor, together with the offshore islands, was settled by emigrants from the mainland of Greece. Those who occupied the most northerly part of this coastal strip were speakers of Aeolic Greek, and those in the south, of Doric; in between, in a region stretching about a hundred miles from north to south, Greeks speaking the Ionic dialect established themselves. This last group of settlers will be referred to as 'the Ionians' (though, strictly speaking, some mainland Greeks were also Ionians); their part of the Asiatic coastline came to be called 'Ionia'. It was in Ionia that Presocratic thought began, and it is remarkable that almost all the thinkers who count as Presocratic were Ionians by birth or descent.

In the Greek world of the tenth and ninth centuries, there was little fine craftsmanship and no originality or distinction in the visual arts. For history there were the stories of the doings of princes of the Mycenean age, preserved and recited by professional singers. The Greeks of this time looked back with a conviction that they had declined, perhaps irrecoverably, from a splendid past. Their political organisation seems to be reflected in the Homeric poems: a multitude of petty princes, who lead their people in battle and administer justice, whose wealth is derived from the ownership of land and who struggle against the encroachments of other noble families. The religion and mythology of the Greeks, so far as it can be reconstructed, was again still basically Mycenean, though even in Mycenean times, and more so later, oriental elements were incorporated. But archaic Greek mythology contained no wide cosmogonical and cosmological speculations such as had appeared much earlier in the thinking of the older civilisations of the Near East. It was focused intently on the individualities of the various gods, on their characteristic activities and spheres of activity. The same love of sharp outlines and definite boundaries can be seen in what there is of Greek art at this period.

The archaeological evidence shows that in Ionia the eighth century was still a period of consolidation. There was not much interaction with Greek or barbarian neighbours. The artefacts produced were not of great distinction compared with those of the same period from mainland Greece, let alone the Near East. But from around 700 on, there was a decisive change, or set of changes, mutually interrelated. The causes of change were operating everywhere else in the Greek world as well, but the effects were particularly notable in Ionia.

The most obvious sign of change was the rapid increase in foreign trade. Territorial expansion was blocked by the rise of the kingdom of Lydia in the hinterland, but the Ionians, with the city of Miletus in the lead, began now to trade intensively all over the eastern Mediterranean, and to plant colonies in favourable places. Together with this, a general turning outwards becomes apparent. The Greeks began to show themselves, in the visual arts at least, able to assimilate the craftsmanship and the conceptions of other cultures and themselves to produce original works of the highest quality. At this period, in the case of those arts of which the products can be recovered by excavation, the barbarians were the teachers and the Greeks generally their apt pupils; which makes it reasonable to expect non-Greek influence in the less material aspects of culture also.

The barbarians available for inspection by an interested Ionian of the seventh and sixth centuries were peoples of pronounced and contrasting individualities, 'barbarian', mostly, only in the sense of 'non-Greek', not in that of 'less civilised'. The Ionians were deeply impressed, both by the variety of these cultures and by their particular attainments. A brief account must be given of these neighbours and of what they had to contribute to the beginnings of Greek thought.

The Scythians, north of the Black Sea, became well known to the Ionians during the seventh century. They deserve mention here because there is evidence of shamanistic beliefs and practices among them, and it now seems certain that some of what is recorded of Pythagoras and other sixth-century Greeks shows that they had acquired some shamanistic lore, probably by way of Scythia and neighbouring Thrace. In Asia Minor, the Lydians and their neighbours the Phrygians were more accessible, but contributed little. These two kingdoms impressed the Ionians by their great wealth and luxury, but besides new forms of music the Greeks learnt from them only the use of coinage, first minted by the Lydians around 600.

During the seventh century the Assyrians were the greatest power in the Near East, and for the first third of the sixth century the Babylonians, before the rise of Persia. The Ionians, with other Greeks, traded into parts of these empires and their art was, undeniably, greatly stimulated by such contact. This was an area in which urban civilisation, and literacy (though restricted to certain classes), were already many centuries old. Here, if any-where, one might expect to find sources of intellectual fertilisa-tion, and they can indeed be found, with some degree of pro-ability, in mathematics, in astronomy and in stories about the origins of the gods and the world.

Babylonian mathematical knowledge can be shown to have reached its highest level around 1600, and to have remained at that level, apparently immobile, for more than a thousand years. Its practitioners never freed themselves from the conception of mathematics as a collection of procedures for finding solutions to possible practical problems. As a result the possibility of abstract-ion from particular problems, which is the life-blood of true math-ematics, was never seen. The contrast with the Greek development is striking, and instructive. Whether or not the Greeks began by borrowing from Babylonia in this field, which is plausible but not provable, they developed, within two hundred years (500 to 300) two branches of pure mathematics, elementary number theory and Euclidean geometry, creating in the process the notions of *axiom, theorem, definition* and *proof*.

Babylonian astronomy, which seems to have begun from the systematic observation of heavenly bodies for purposes of ritual and divination, had by 600 accumulated a large corpus of empir-ical data, and had discovered a number of simple rules governing some celestial phenomena. These rules might be applied to the future to produce something like a prediction. The transmission of Babylonian astronomical knowledge to the Greeks is an obscure and controversial subject, but it cannot be avoided in any study of the Presocratics. If some transmission in the sixth century can be established, this will be important not merely as showing that some sixth-century Greeks (and therefore very likely the earliest Presocratics) were interested in astronomy, but also because it will be the more probable that sixth-century Greek cosmology also owed something to Babylon. These problems will be considered again in the next chapter.

The Phoenicians and the related peoples of the Syrian coast occupied in the Ancient Near East a position which has often been compared to a crossroads. Much Babylonian influence must have been transmitted to the Greeks through this region, in which they appear as traders and adventurers from the ninth century onwards. It is more difficult to judge of the original contributions of Phoenicians and Canaanites, but their craftsmanship in many visual arts certainly enriched Greek art, and the tablets found at Ras Shamra reveal a store of properly Canaanite myth and legend. It may well be that there were movements of thought in Phoenicia at this time which were directly influential on the earliest Presocratics. This suggestion cannot be either proved or disproved in the present state of knowledge, but it receives some support both from the Phoenician cosmogonies (for which see Chapter Two) and from some more general considerations which will be pointed out later in this chapter. The alphabet, which the Greeks certainly owed to the Phoenicians, was itself an innovation of profound importance for Ionia and Greece generally; this too is discussed below.

Finally, Egypt. This peculiar country stimulated the Greek imagination, and there was a persistent belief among the Greeks themselves that Egypt above all other lands was the repository of ancient wisdom. In spite of this, and though many Ionian and other Greeks visited Egypt in the seventh and sixth centuries as merchants or mercenaries, the provable cultural debts are few

outside the visual arts where Egyptian influence was great. Mathematics and astronomy were in Egypt on a lower level than in
Babylonia; medicine was much more highly developed, and it
is possible that medical knowledge was transmitted to Greece. As
in Babylon, so in Egypt there were theological and cosmogonical
speculations, which were often clearly influenced by Babylonian
ideas on the same subject.

To this brief survey of Ionian horizons in the seventh and
early sixth centuries must be added something about the Iranian
peoples, the Medes and the Persians. These began in the sixth
century to extend their joint power westwards from what is now
Iran, so rapidly that by 540 they were masters of the whole of
Asia Minor, including the Greek cities of the coast, having
crushed the Babylonian empire and the Lydian kingdom in the
process. It is important to remember that they can hardly have been
known to the Ionians much before 550. The Ionians were fascinated by their strange new masters; it was a novel experience for
them to form a peripheral part of a vast empire. What was more,
the Iranian people had their own ideas about the gods, both
traditional and new. Zoroaster, who seems to have lived around
600, reinterpreted the traditional Iranian religion in the light of
his personal revelation to found a simple and sober monotheism.
His teachings spread through the growing Persian empire, and at
the end of the sixth century King Darius himself in his inscriptions made a Zoroastrian confession of faith. There is every likelihood therefore that Iranian religion was both familiar and
appealing to many Ionians of the later sixth century. Iranian
influence may well have been more decisive and important for
Ionian thought than Babylonian or any other. It must be remembered, though, that the evidence about early Iranian religion
consists mostly of texts of a much later date, written after that
religion had undergone many changes and had in turn been
subject to Greek influences. It is therefore necessary to be very
cautious in claiming to find Iranian influence in early Greek
thought.

*

The Greeks of early Ionia cannot but have been afflicted with a consciousness of their own newness, immaturity and lack of achievement in comparison with some of the other civilisations they saw. But this is not to say that they were overwhelmed by foreign influences. In some of the visual arts it is possible to trace their development step by step, and to observe that everywhere the Greek artists succeed in assimilating what other cultures offer and in creating nevertheless something original of their own. In poetry, foreign influence was never significant at all. The Homeric poems, the *Iliad* and the *Odyssey*, were composed from traditional Greek material, probably in the eighth century, by one or two Ionian poets. They show that by 700 Ionian culture could already produce great poetry of the highest technical accomplishment. It was already clear by that date that Greek literature was not, and would never be, anything but wholly Greek. All this may be relevant when we consider the foreign debts of the early Presocratics.

If Ionia already in 700 had a cultural individuality, this became even more true during the next hundred and fifty years. The great expansion in trade, and the beginning of colonisation, have been mentioned. These changes were linked, in ways that are not always clear, with others: the advent of the alphabet, a political development which was something new in the history of the world, the rise of a city-state ethos, and a general increase in awareness and the application of intelligence to things. All of these changes are important in accounting for the origin of Presocratic thought, and something must be said about each.

The Phoenicians and other North Semitic peoples had been using alphabetic scripts since far back in the second millennium. The Greek alphabet was adapted from the Phoenician at some time probably not far distant from 800, when regular commercial contacts had been established; but the use of alphabetic writing does not seem to have become general in any Greek territory for another century. It seems possible that the Greek alphabet was at first used only by merchants to keep their records, and perhaps even remained a trade secret for some time. By 700, however, it

was becoming important in other parts of life. The conception of
the *Iliad* and the *Odyssey* as we know them is hardly thinkable
without the notion of a standard text made possible by writing;
still less is the highly personal poetry of Hesiod, Archilochus and
the early lyric poets. (Prose works do not appear till the sixth
century, with the first Presocratics and Pherecydes of Syros.) Yet
another possibility opened up was that of the rationalisation,
standardisation and publication of law, which was to be a great
and perhaps decisive factor in the political development of
Greece, and important for the Presocratics also.

The political development of the Greek cities can be followed
in broad outline, since in many cities it was clearly very similar.
By the eighth century the royal families had generally lost most
of their power to small groups of nobles. In the next two centuries
the position of the aristocrats was in its turn eroded by the increase of mercantile wealth and the introduction of the hoplite
style of warfare, which gave a decisive power in the city to the increasing numbers of well-to-do citizens outside the nobility. The
hoplite citizens—those who could afford the suit of heavy armour
required—usually gained political power by backing a single
leader who then executed a *coup d'état* and ruled with their co-
operation; the standard name for a leader of this kind was 'tyrant'
(*turannos*) which did not then have the sinister connotations
which it has since acquired. Tyrants begin to appear in the
seventh century in mainland Greece; in Ionia the development
was probably a few decades later.

The appearance of written laws in the seventh century goes
naturally together with this stage of political evolution. In the
kingly and aristocratic regimes, law had been unwritten and was
administered, by reference to inherited tradition, by the hereditary rulers. This kind of jurisdiction was likely to prove unfit to
meet the needs of merchants, who would begin to require a
definite and relatively sophisticated code governing property and
contracts; but above all it placed indefinite power in the hands of
those who sat, by birthright, in judgment. The age of the tyrants
is the age of the lawgivers—one man must often have been both

—in which publicly accessible codes of law and constitutions were created.

Written law-codes were no new thing in the history of the world; what *was* new was that these codes were not imposed from above, but were the expression of the political will of a considerable section of the citizen body, and must have commanded the consent of a majority of citizens. For the first time in human history, it seems, communities of men were regulated by impartial rules which they themselves had deliberately chosen and assented to, and which could be discussed and altered with the consent of the majority. This was a decisive step even though it would be wrong to speak of 'democracy' (rather it was—disregarding the tyrants—broadly-based oligarchy; women, slaves, and in most cases the poorer citizens had no effective say). And an alphabetic script was necessary for the laws to be made generally accessible.

It will be suggested in the next chapter that the political evolution which has just been outlined was a necessary condition or at least an important factor for the origin of Presocratic thought. If this is right, it is interesting to ask why such an evolution had not occurred anywhere previously. The prerequisites seem to include: an alphabetic script, a fairly general distribution of wealth, and a sense of belonging to a natural community, upon the welfare of which one's own welfare closely depended. These prerequisites were perhaps not present previously except in the Phoenician cities; of these, those in the Levant fell under the overlordship of Assyria in the ninth century, while still ruled by kings, but Carthage seems to have evolved towards a broad oligarchy in the same way as the Greek cities, though not earlier than they. Of early Phoenician legal codes nothing is known and of developments in Phoenicia parallel to the Presocratics there is little evidence, which will be mentioned in Chapter Two.

Ionia was not particularly advanced in its political development. Hoplite warfare was adopted there, as the alphabet had been, rather later than in mainland Greece. There was also the

complication that some Ionian cities were intermittently subject
to Lydia between 700 and 550. But Miletus and Samos remained
independent of Lydia and commercially prosperous. The recorded history of Miletus begins with the tyranny of Thrasybulus,
followed early in the sixth century by an unusually prolonged
and frightful civil war, which, however, does not seem to have
seriously affected its prosperity.

Less tangible currents of thought and feeling should be mentioned here, though they cannot be properly discussed. The
political and social changes brought into being an urban society.
Loyalties to hereditary chieftains, to clan and to family, were
slowly weakened, and replaced by loyalty to the citizen body as a
whole, or to a particular class of citizens. The focus of mental
culture was the marketplace or the harbour, where ideas and
news, as well as goods, were freely exchanged. There was a
growing dissatisfaction with traditional religion, as unable to
satisfy new spiritual needs, and with traditional sources of information about the world. In the lyric poets of the seventh and sixth
centuries, the individual personality became for the first time
something of primary interest and value. For much of this,
suggestive parallels can be fetched from the early Middle Ages.
There was, certainly, what may be described as a general increase
in awareness and in the application of intelligence to the world.

CHAPTER TWO

The Milesians

THE *Theogony* of Hesiod is very likely the earliest work of Greek literature that we possess. Its author lived in Boeotia, on the Greek mainland, and can be plausibly dated to near the beginning of the seventh century. The *Theogony* is an attempt to construct a unified genealogy of the gods. It is far from being merely a re-working of traditional Greek stories. The chief deities of the Greeks have a prominent place; but the story which looms largest—the 'Succession Myth', in which Uranus is deposed by his son Cronus who is in turn succeeded by his son Zeus—is of Near Eastern origin, though it had perhaps arrived in Greece in the Mycenean age. What is more, the well-known gods are surrounded by a host of others not often, or not all, worshipped by Greeks, and in many cases 'invented' by Hesiod himself. These others correspond to features of the universe which Hesiod thought important: we find such diverse divinities as Earth, Night, Rivers, Sleep, Strife, Victory, and so on. Hesiod is not personifying or allegorising; he believes in the existence of all his gods alike. What is important is that he is led to assert their existence, and to assign them a particular place in his genealogy, only partly on the strength of mere tradition. Usually, the deficiencies of tradition are supplied or corrected by Hesiod from considerations of what is reasonable. Sleep, for instance, is clearly an important god; it is reasonable that he should appear in the genealogy, and clearly reasonable that he should figure as the son of Night.

What Hesiod does in the *Theogony* is like Presocratic thought in many ways. He attempts to create a complete, unified and

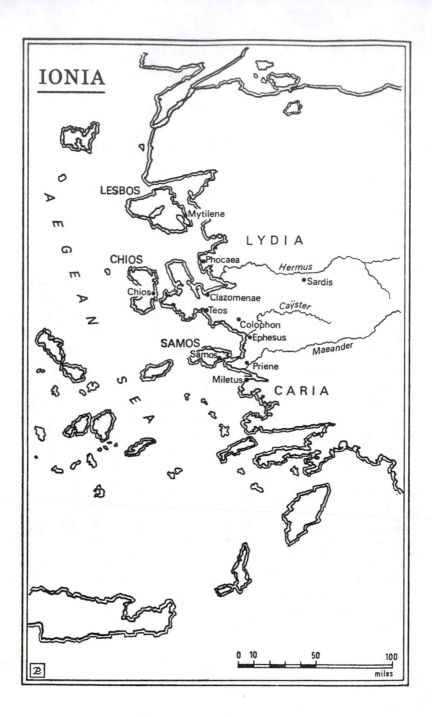

IONIA

LESBOS
Mytilene

LYDIA

CHIOS
Phocaea
Hermus
Sardis

Chios
Clazomenae
Teos
Caÿster
Colophon
Ephesus
SAMOS
Maeander
Samos
Priene
Miletus
CARIA

A E G E A N   S E A

0   10   50   100
miles

reasonable picture of the workings and history of the universe. He employs a single basic mechanism (the begetting of gods by gods) to achieve this picture. He is by no means constrained by tradition, and he is open to non-Greek ideas. Yet between Hesiod and even the earliest Presocratics there is a great gulf, created by a revolution in thought.

In order to see more clearly what this revolution was, it will be helpful to move on nearly two hundred years to look at the theological opinions of Xenophanes of Colophon, an Ionian born about the mid-sixth century. Xenophanes is probably not an original thinker, but he is important because the surviving fragments of his works contain the first certain statements of a theology which in sixth-century Greece was new and revolutionary:

One god there is, greatest among gods and men,* in no way like mortal creatures either in bodily form or in the thought of his mind (fr. 23).

The whole of him sees, the whole of him thinks, the whole of him hears (fr. 24).

He stays always motionless in the same place; it is not fitting that he should move about now this way, now that (fr. 26).

But, effortlessly, he wields all things by the thought of his mind (fr. 25).

Corresponding to these positive statements, there is sharp criticism of traditional views, including those of Hesiod:

But mortal men imagine that gods are begotten, and that they have human dress and speech and shape (fr. 14).

If oxen or horses or lions had hands to draw with and to make works of art as men do, then horses would draw the forms of gods like horses, oxen like oxen, and they would make their gods' bodies similar to the bodily shape that they themselves each had (fr. 15).

The Ethiopians say their gods are snub-nosed and black-skinned, the Thracians that they are blue-eyed and red-headed (fr. 16).

Homer and Hesiod have attributed to the gods everything which brings shame and reproach among men: theft, adultery and fraud (fr. 11).

* 'Among gods and men' is a way of speaking: it does not imply the existence of other gods.

For the source of this radical monotheism, so foreign to the traditional Greek religion, it is reasonable to look first to the Near East. There seem to have been monotheistic tendencies both in Iranian and in Hebrew religious thought at this time as well as in Greece itself. Yet whether or not any inspiration came from these quarters, Xenophanes' theology is still something quite new. In attacking head-on the traditional beliefs and putting forward utterly different ones, Xenophanes makes no appeal to the authority of a prophet or teacher, still less to any personal revelation. He relies entirely on certain general principles—certain conceptions of what it is reasonable or fitting that a god should be. Further indications of this way of argument are preserved in other reports about Xenophanes: he argued, for instance, that it cannot be that one god is ruler of other gods (as in traditional religion), since it was 'contrary to divine law' that gods should have masters.

This way of thinking, it must be repeated, was something quite new. For the first time, a conscious and deliberate attempt had been made to set up a standard of what was and was not 'reasonable' or 'fitting' in theology. Everything was to be judged in terms of this standard alone, and the authority of tradition, or of a general consensus, or of a great teacher, was to count for nothing. By the application of this method, a doctrine of great generality and coherence was produced.

Xenophanes will be considered again in the next chapter. He has been introduced here, out of turn, because it is by working back from his fragments that one may best hope to understand the intellectual atmosphere of the earliest Presocratics, the thinkers of sixth-century Miletus.

Something of the political and social development of early Ionia has been sketched in the last chapter. Miletus, commercially the leading city, shared in these developments as well as being particularly accessible to Near Eastern influence. What seems especially important for the revolution in thought is the emergence of the concept of *law* as something determinate, impartial, and unchanging, and the spread of political equality. A debate between equals, in the popular assembly or the law-courts, must be conducted by appeals to general, impartial principles of law or reason—otherwise the parties will not be equal. The notion of 'reasoned argument' will begin to develop. There will grow up a habit of seeing particular situations as applications of a superior, abstract law. And law of this kind will be seen as the necessary arbiter of any complex whole in which order is apparent.

In this way, the new kind of thinking apparent in Xenophanes can be plausibly linked with the equally new political and social developments of seventh- and sixth-century Greece. One would expect the Milesian thinkers to fit into the same sort of context. As far as can be seen from the evidence, which is sparse and difficult to interpret, they fit extremely well. What follows is a reconstruction of Milesian thought which tries to take account of the evidence but which necessarily goes beyond it in places, and which is guided by the ideas which have been outlined.

Over some period in the first seventy years of the sixth century was spread the active life of three citizens of Miletus: Thales, Anaximander and Anaximenes, of whom Anaximenes was at least slightly younger than the first two. Hardly anything is known about the lives of these men. They must have been known to one another, and it is reliably reported that Thales and Anaximander were close associates. These three produced the systems of ideas about the nature of the universe which, at least since Aristotle, have been recognised as a new beginning. Anaximander and Anaximenes set out their systems in writing—two of the earliest Greek prose treatises—but Thales wrote nothing. In consequence, very little reliable information indeed is to be had about his ideas: our best informant, Aristotle, makes it clear that what evidence he could find was meagre and at second hand; at best, it came from the other Milesians. Before the three are considered separately, the main lines of the 'Milesian' view of the universe will be given. If an opinion or idea is described, in what follows, as 'Milesian', this will mean that it appears in Anaximander or Anaximenes and was, for all we can tell, common to all three thinkers.

*

For the theological beliefs of the Milesians, the only reliable direct evidence is in a passage of Aristotle's *Physics* (203^b 3–15). This suggests that the early natural philosophers, and Anaximander in particular, held that there was a single boundless all-powerful and immortal divinity which encompassed and controlled the universe. A theology of this kind would be close to that of Xenophanes, and it is reasonable to suppose that the arguments by which it was supported were similar.

It is clear that this kind of theology, supported by this kind of argument, will have far-reaching consequences for cosmology. The method of Hesiod's *Theogony*, in particular, will no longer be an acceptable way of producing a coherent account of the structure and workings of the universe. Since these are now dependent on the power of the unique supreme god, it is necessary to discover, if possible, the ways in which that power is exercised; to discover, therefore, the plan upon which God controls the universe. There were those who thought the enterprise hopeless: the mind of God was inscrutable and of infinite complexity, so that the order of the universe was inexplicable by man. This was the belief, for example, of the author of the book of Job, in the fifth century, and, in Greece of the same period, of the poet Pindar, whose poetry is permeated by a feeling for the sheer irreducible complexity of phenomena both physical and mental. The Milesians were of another mind: they supposed, equally with some support from observed facts, that the universe, being controlled by a supreme divinity worthy of the name, must necessarily be a universe of order, of lawlike regularity, and of intellectually satisfying construction. To hold this belief inevitably inclines men to be naïvely optimistic and to underrate the subtlety of nature. Their constructions are doomed always to turn out crude by comparison with reality. As Pindar said, 'They pluck the fruit of wisdom when it is unripe' (fr. 197 Bowra, 209 Snell), and with these words he dismissed the first century of Presocratic thought. The sneer, coming from Pindar, is no cheap one; but it applies if at all to the whole history of all sciences, not only to the first Presocratics.

The problems that most concerned the Milesians can be reduced to the question: what are the relations between the supreme power in the universe, 'the Divine', and the observable world-order? The Milesians aimed to find an answer which would square both with the observed facts and with what they held to be necessarily true about the supreme god.

The observable world-order is, for them, a bounded system of earth, sea, murky lower atmosphere, translucent sky, and the heavenly bodies, together, probably, with a hard outer shell to which the fixed stars may have been thought to be attached. This system behaves, in broad outline, with regularity, the principal changes repeating themselves in daily and yearly cycles. These easily observable cycles must have been the best guarantee for the Milesians of the existence of a controlling law in the universe: the parallel with the periodic rotation of political office necessary among equals was close at hand. Beyond this system, and unlike it *not* bounded in space or in time, is 'the Unbounded' (*to apeiron*) which is the supreme divinity and controls the whole universe. Being alive, it is perpetually in motion.

This concept of 'the Unbounded' is so important that something more must be said about its history and significance. The word *apeiron* is a negative adjective in the neuter formed from the noun *peirar* or *peras*. This noun has various applications in early Greek, most of which can be summed up by saying that the *peras* of X is that which completes X in some respect or marks the completion of X. So '*to apeiron*' is 'that which cannot be completed', without any necessary specialisation to a spatial or a temporal sense. But the spatial and temporal senses were the most natural for it to bear at this time, namely, 'spatially unbounded' and 'unending in time'.

The most obvious role of 'the Unbounded' in the Milesian scheme was that of sustaining the observed world-order. What is beyond the edge of the observable region, and why does everything not fall down? The Unbounded is 'outside' and keeps the world-order in its place. What keeps the orderly cycle of change going, and moves the heavenly bodies in their courses? The

Unbounded, which never gives out, supplies the necessary motive power. In giving such answers to such questions, the Milesians were looking at the observed world-order 'from outside', and contrasting its finitude in space and time with the boundlessness of God. This contrast is encapsulated in another important word, *kosmos* (plural: *kosmoi*). As a technical term, meaning a 'world-system' containing the components of the visible world-order, this was current in the fifth century, and there is no reason why it should not have been coined in this sense by the Milesians, who would certainly have felt the need for a term of this meaning.

To look at our *kosmos* from the outside is to become aware that it may be not the only *kosmos* in the universe. The Milesians almost certainly held that there existed at any time an unlimited number of *kosmoi*, dotted about in the Unbounded, and their reasoning has probably been preserved by Aristotle (*Physics* 203^b 25–8), though he does not attribute it: if there is a *kosmos* here, in the Unbounded, then why not elsewhere, since there are no privileged places in the Unbounded? It is an appeal to the equality under cosmic law of all places in the universe, or (as we should say) to the principle of Sufficient Reason, of which Anaximander made striking use in another connection (see below).

A *kosmos*, by contrast with the Unbounded, was essentially not divine, though it was produced by creation by and from the Unbounded; it was finite, both in space and in time, having both an origin and an end. Here the obvious problem is to explain how a *kosmos* is created and how it is kept going, agreeably with the observed facts and with theology. All the Milesians were concerned with this problem, and gave different answers which can be partly reconstructed with greater or less probability. It becomes necessary to take them one by one.

Thales, the first Milesian thinker, was obviously a remarkable figure in public life, who by the fifth century had become legendary as a man of practical ingenuity. About his ideas, as has been explained, hardly anything can be counted certain. All that is possible is more or less plausible speculation, which must begin from the reports of Aristotle (esp. *Metaphysics* 983^b 20–7) that Thales was the 'pioneer' of natural philosophy, that he was said to have held that water was the origin of all things, and that the earth was supported by water. The emergence of the whole universe from an original mass of water, and a cosmic scheme in which there are waters both below the earth and above the firmament, are ideas which appear throughout the ancient Near East, and no doubt Thales drew from that source. But it is still necessary to explain why he took up these particular Near Eastern ideas, and what he used them for. Here a suggestion of Aristotle seems relevant. What water is needed for is life, and the dependence of life upon water is starkly obvious to every inhabitant of the Mediterranean region. This would indicate that Thales was primarily concerned to account for the life in the universe, and in particular the motive power that created the *kosmos* and kept it going. Another scrap of evidence says that Thales equated being alive with the possession of motive power, and, applying this principle, concluded that lodestones were living things (Aristotle, *de Anima* 405^a 19–21). Water, then, may have been identified as the fuel or the mover of the universe; things in the *kosmos* that could cause change had originated from water and retained its properties, some more than others. That even hot and dry things might be 'nourished' by water was suggested by the idea that the sun draws up water from the sea to feed itself—this idea was certainly current in the fifth century. And that moisture could create even dry and solid things was suggested not only by the facts of animal reproduction, but by the apparent turning of the sea to dry land at Miletus itself—a phenomenon due to the deposition of silt by the river Maeander.

This is at best conjecture, and any suggestions about the theological ideas of Thales must be equally conjectural. Aristotle (*de Anima* 411^a 8) attributes to him the saying 'all things are full of gods', which suggests that he was prepared to regard all forces in nature as equally divine—a view which would clearly fit in with the derivation of all forces from a divine wateriness.

Such speculations about Thales are not entirely in the air. They derive some degree of confirmation from what can be known of Anaximander, the friend of Thales. About Anaximander's opinions there is at least evidence which can be presumed reliable, within limits, derived from two witnesses, Aristotle and Theophrastus, who had read the book in which Anaximander had set down these opinions. This evidence is still very difficult to handle: it is often hard to separate what Aristotle and Theophrastus found in Anaximander's book from the interpretation they put upon it. For such reasons, there is wide divergence of opinion about fundamental questions in Anaximander. The following account is put, for convenience of exposition, rather dogmatically; much is controversial, as may be seen from any of the books referred to in the notes.

The foundation of Anaximander's system, as has been said, was the contrast between the Unbounded and the world-systems (*kosmoi*). Now for Anaximander the most important forces at work in the *kosmoi* were what were later called 'the opposites': pairs of opposed entities of which the most frequently invoked were 'the hot' and 'the cold', 'the wet' and 'the dry'. These were conceived of neither precisely as substances nor precisely as qualities, these distinctions being post-Socratic. The 'opposites' were above all *forces*, agents of physical change, each present in varying degrees at different places. There is no reason to think that Anaximander went beyond ordinary observation in what he said about the relations of these 'opposites' to such obvious constituents of the world as earth or water or fire. There is, further, every reason to suppose that he did not make clear in any precise way the relation of the 'opposites' to the Unbounded out of which they came. For if he had done so, Aristotle and Theophrastus would not have been as puzzled as they were about how to fit him in to their own scheme of classification. The Aristotelian scheme of classification of previous 'physical speculators' (*phusiologoi*) demanded that something like the Aristotelian concept of 'material cause' should have been in the minds of those classified. It was then possible to ask whether a particular thinker had taken the universe to contain one or more material causes. Anaximander might be pressed in either direction. Aristotle himself takes, in two places (*Physics* 187ᵃ 20–1; *Metaphysics* 1069ᵇ 18–24), the view that Anaximander's Unbounded (taken to be the material cause of what was in the universe) was meant to be a mixture of all the 'opposites', which Aristotle seems to have thought of as playing the role of material causes in Anaximander's system. Yet Aristotle noticeably does not venture to include this interpretation of Anaximander in the first book of the *Metaphysics*, which contains his most considered remarks on the early thinkers. And Theophrastus (DK 12 A 9ᵃ) recognised (as it seems) that there was not sufficient evidence to decide between this interpretation and another one, according to which all the 'opposites' were simply modifications of the Unbounded, and there was only one material cause, namely the Unbounded itself, whatever that might be.

The difficulty in which Aristotle and Theophrastus found themselves in trying to classify Anaximander is instructive in several ways. It is an excellent example of the classic pitfall in the history of philosophy, conceptual anachronism. It shows the limitations of Aristotle as a historian of thought. Again, the vagueness of Anaximander on the point at issue shows that not merely the Aristotelian concept of 'material cause' but even a more informal concept of 'matter' or 'material substance' was as yet not in use, and thereby sets in relief the achievements of Anaximenes, Heraclitus and their successors in working forwards to such a concept. Those to whom it seems paradoxical that the notion of a thing's 'matter' or 'substance' should be less immediate than that of its origin or past history should look at the questions that God puts to Job out of the whirlwind (Job chs. 38 and 39). These are good examples of the kinds of question that would be put to the Presocratics. Many are about the origins and motive powers of things, none about their 'matter' or 'substance'.

It does not follow that Anaximander said nothing about the relation of the 'opposites' to the Unbounded, only that he is likely to have concentrated on saying how the opposites came out of the Unbounded to create a world-system. For this part of

Anaximander's account there is some evidence, though as usual it is difficult to interpret and coordinate it. We are told that the cause of the separation-out of the 'opposites' was the perpetual movement of the Unbounded. This is very vague, and the report (in DK 12 A 9) is of doubtful standing. Firmer ground is provided by indications in Aristotle (esp. *de Caelo* 295ª 9–14) that a 'whirl' (*dinē*), a vortex movement, was important in the creation of a *kosmos*. It looks as if the *dinē* was used to explain both the separation of the *kosmos* into heavy and light components and the circlings of the heavenly bodies. When water containing particles of varying kinds has been stirred in a bowl, the heavier particles tend to sink and to congregate about the axis of rotation, while the lighter ones execute their revolutions higher up and further from the axis. On this model it was posible to account for the formation of the earth 'below' and the movements of heavenly bodies 'above'. Whether the 'whirl' had the more general function of separating out the 'opposites' is uncertain. It seems unlikely in view of the other evidence. A doxographical fragment derived from Theophrastus gives this account of the first stage of cosmogony:

He [Anaximander] says that, at the origin of this world-system, that which, coming from the Eternal, was generative of hot and cold was separated off, and that this produced a kind of ball of flame which formed around the mist in the region of the earth, like the bark around a tree (A10).

If the simile of the tree and its bark goes back to Anaximander, as seems probable, he was being guided here by an analogy with the formation of living things. The word 'generative' (*gonimon*) points in the same direction. In addition to these clues, there is the general reflection that for the creation of a *kosmos* from the Unbounded it is difficult to think of any natural analogy except from animal reproduction, and that Thales may have used analogies of this kind. All this suggests that the origin and development of a *kosmos* may have been thought of as like that of an egg or an embryo. The idea that this *kosmos* began as a 'world-egg' certainly appears in 'Orphic' poems which are probably later than Anaximander and in the comic cosmogony in Aristophanes' *Birds*, not to mention certain Hindu scriptures in which an original deity impregnates itself. More generally, an analogy between the *kosmos* and an animal was taken seriously by several thinkers of the Presocratic period, as will be seen.

It must not be thought that there was any essential conflict for Anaximander between the 'mechanical' model of the *dinē* and the 'biological' model of the egg or embryo. Anaximander was not committed to explaining exclusively by analogies of one sort or another, and did not (in all probability) press any of his analogies very hard. Even in the last Presocratics the process of cosmogony is explained only in rather vague, intuitive terms. Yet the inherent disparity between biological and mechanical explanation was to become a source of confusion.

In the developed *kosmos*, the working of each of the 'opposites' is thought of as a continual struggle against its opposed twin. Each gains ground at certain times in certain places, and loses ground correspondingly at other times and places. It is natural to ask whether these gains and losses involved the transformation of one 'opposite' into another, the destruction of one by another, or merely the advance of one 'opposite' and the retreat of the other. Theophrastus seems to have asked this question, and to have answered it by claiming that Anaximander's 'opposites' turned into one another. Unfortunately, the passage derived from his report on which this conclusion is based does not suggest that Theophrastus had any very strong grounds for his claim. The passage runs as follows:

[Anaximander says that] the destruction of things that are takes place by their turning back into those things from which they had their origin, *according to necessity*; for they *make requital and recompense* to one another for their injustice, according to the *assessment of Time*. (Such are the rather poetical phrases he uses in speaking of them) (A9 and B1).

This passage cannot well refer to anything except the struggle of the 'opposites', and if so it is evidence that Theophrastus saw this struggle as a succession of transformations, but does not explain why. It may very well be that Theophrastus' reasons have been lost in abridgement.

Nevertheless, this passage is still very intersting. The comment at the end shows that at least some of the less prosaic expressions used were quoted by Theophrastus from Anaximander's book. It follows that the phrases rendered by the words italicised above are probably Anaximander's own phrases. They bring us back to the problem of how the Unbounded controls the events in each *kosmos*, and thus to the idea of the *kosmos* as governed by law. It is clear that 'injustice' consists in the encroachment by one 'opposite' on the other, and that the 'requital' is the restitution of the unjust gains and a corresponding loss as well. There is an overall regulation of the fight; however it may go in small areas of space and time, it is evened up in the long run over the whole *kosmos*, the cycles of day and night, and of the seasons, being the most obvious evidence for the existence of such a law. This law is not guaranteed by some inherent equipollence of forces, but imposed externally, by the intervention of the Unbounded. This at least is the most reasonable conclusion from various indications. We know in general that the Unbounded 'governs' the universe, and so is the natural source of physical law. Moreover, the lawlike behaviour occurs 'by necessity' (*kata to chreōn*), which implies a power imposing the necessity, and 'according to the assessment of Time' (*kata tēn tou chronou taxin*). The significance of this last phrase is, unfortunately, disputable, but it is quite possible that 'Time' is here thought of as the name of a divine power, namely the Unbounded. For the idea of Time as a divine power occurs, not only in Iranian religion, but in other Greek sixth-century writers: Solon, Pherecydes and Heraclitus.

Each *kosmos* lasted only a finite time, but on the later stages of its existence there is no direct information. Presumably it aged like an animal or ran down like a clock, the rotatory movement which was its life and gave it its form slowing down and eventually stopping, whereupon its contents would be reabsorbed into the Unbounded.

Within this grandiose framework, Anaximander filled in a great number of smaller details about our *kosmos* as it now is. Here is a list of some of the questions to which he offered answers (it is again worth while to compare Job chs. 38 and 39): how the heavenly bodies were formed; at what distances they are from the earth; what is the cause of eclipses; why the earth remains in the same place; what is the shape of the earth; what are the causes of winds, rain, thunder, lightning, earthquakes and the annual flooding of the Nile; what was the origin of animals and mankind. He also constructed a map of the earth's surface. Space does not allow treatment of all these details, but two points of particular significance must be mentioned here.

One is the explanation of why the earth remains in the same place. This problem, as Aristotle remarks, exercised all the Presocratics, just as it did many other people. With the single exception of Anaximander, all the early Presocratics (and most later ones) supposed that the earth had some material support: a pillar of solid earth (Xenophanes) or a cushion of air (Anaximenes) or water (Thales), on which it floated. Anaximander appealed instead to symmetry. There was no reason why the earth should move downwards rather than in any other direction, since it was symmetrically placed in the middle of the *kosmos*. This explanation might seem to imply that Anaximander took both earth and *kosmos* to be spherical; in fact we know that his earth was cylindrical, as befitted the product of a cosmic vortex. The appeal to symmetry may therefore have proceeded in two stages rather than in one, using first a symmetry about a horizontal plane through the earth, and secondly a radial symmetry around the axis of the cosmic rotation. If this is right, he ought in consistency to have maintained that the flat surface of the earth which, relatively to us, was the under surface, exhibited the same features as the 'upper' surface—rivers, mountains, animals and so on; and that there was correspondingly another set of heavenly bodies 'below'. A faint trace of this doctrine appears in the doxography.

In any case, this explanation is the earliest certain instance of an appeal to the principle of Sufficient Reason—a principle which, as has been suggested, is characteristic of the spirit of Milesian cosmology.

The second important point of detail is Anaximander's account of the origin of animal and human life on the earth. Animals, including human beings, he supposed to have been originally produced by spontaneous generation from mud, by the action of the sun's heat on moist earth. Of the beginnings of the human race he held a remarkable theory, which was clearly designed to take account of the fact that the new-born human infant is unable to fend for itself. The prototypes of human beings were originally produced as fish-like creatures, encased in a spiny bark, and inhabiting the water; in due course, on reaching maturity, they took to the dry land and shed their fish-like exterior, emerging in human form. This striking 'anticipation' of modern theories of human phylogeny suggest that Anaximander may have known something of the development of the human embryo. If so, this would add some plausibility to the attempt to find biological analogies in his cosmogony.

Anaximander's system was, naturally, open to objections on points of detail, since it offered solutions to all the problems of cosmology which most interested his contemporaries. It is more important that it was in danger of internal incoherence. Not only did Anaximander give no clear explanation of how the 'opposites' existed in the Unbounded, or of how they alternately prevailed in the *kosmoi*. He left it unexplained how, if everything was regulated by divine law, there could occur even local and temporary 'injustice'. All these difficulties may be comprehended in the general problem: how far is the deity identical with the worlds it creates and governs, how far are they distinct from it?

As soon as Anaximander's ideas were discussed in the spirit in which they were propounded, this question must have begun to emerge. It is therefore not surprising that the main innovation of the third Milesian thinker, Anaximenes, is an attempt at a new kind of answer to the problem. Remaining within the 'Milesian' framework outlined above, Anaximenes declared that the contents of the world-systems that emerge from the Unbounded deity are produced from it, and are interconvertible with it and each other, by processes of condensation and rarefaction. In other words, some notion approximating to that of Aristotle's 'material cause' is invoked or constructed.

This point deserves further precision. If we are to be able to say that Y is the 'same thing' as X, what seems to be required is not merely that X should change into Y in a fairly continuous fashion, but also that this change should be intelligible and lawlike, in other words that it should appear explicable in familiar terms, and should proceed according to definite laws which place restrictions on the ways in which X may change and what it may change into. Further, the change should ideally be reversible, so that X can be recreated from Y; and at any rate we must be able to reidentify in Y those properties of X which we take to be most essential and characteristic of X. All these features can be found in Anaximenes' theory. It is not suggested that he identified each of them, still less that he made a self-conscious conceptual analysis. Rather, the the whole nexus of conditions will have emerged as 'natural' in the circumstances, given the need to produce, within the Milesian framework, a lawlike process of change linking the deity to the *kosmoi*.

If this account is on the right lines, then an essential step in Anaximenes' construction was an appeal to certain facts of experience. Anaximenes seems to have been guided by the observation that the more closely anything is compressed, the harder and more solid it becomes. This suggests that we may explain solid, liquid and gaseous things by the varying degrees of compression of one basic material. It is natural to take as a leading fact here the interconvertibility of water and snow or ice; Anaximenes did so, and stated more generally the principle that heat was associated with expansion or rarefaction, cold with compression or condensation. Going on from this, he constructed a spectrum in which all the main components of our *kosmos* were ranged according to their degree of condensation. The spectrum was: fire, air, wind, cloud, water, earth, rock.

This theory gave each *kosmos* an internal coherence far beyond what it had had for Anaximander. But the internal coherence only reflected the external coherence between the *kosmoi* and the unbounded deity. For Anaximenes gave the deity too a place on the spectrum, by declaring that it existed in the form of air. The consideration that determined this choice was almost certainly the fact that animals must breathe in order to live. This fact had long been connected with the popular conception of the *psuchē* or life-principle as the 'breath of life' which left the body at death. There is in the doxography a report (DK 13 B 2) that Anaximenes made an explicit analogy between the role of *psuchē* in the living body and that of the divine air in the *kosmos*. The report shows clear signs of having been influenced by Stoic ideas, but this does not mean that its kernel is not authentic; the Stoics embroidered the doxography rather than invented it. If this is right, the divine air of Anaximenes is another sign that, for the Milesians, the most characteristic property of the controlling deity was that he was alive and could initiate movement.

This new general theory of physical change was Anaximenes' sole important contribution. It seems unlikely, to judge by the doxography, that he worked it out in much greater detail or made applications of it to particular problems. Some details of his cosmological speculations are preserved, but they bear no obvious relation to the general theory.

This chapter has been focused, up to this point, upon the ideas and attitudes of the Milesian thinkers, with some suggestion of how they are to be related to the political and economic developments sketched in the first chapter. But it is interesting, and may be important, to consider the relations of Milesian thought to the whole intellectual history of the ancient Near East. The very brief survey of Ionian horizons in the first chapter showed, at least, the great variety of possibilities for fruitful transmission of ideas from the barbarians, and especially from the old urban civilisations of the 'Fertile Crescent'. The evidence in detail for such transmission has been growing gradually stronger in the last hundred years as the written records of those civilisations have been unearthed and interpreted. Fresh documents may yet be found which will warrant new conclusions.

If we assume, however, that the evidence so far available is not seriously misleading, and if the view of the Milesians taken in this chapter is correct in general, then it can be said that they were indisputably influenced from the Near East, but that such influence was of an incidental, secondary kind, in a sense to be explained. The core of the Milesian revolution, namely, the development of a reformed theology based on general principles, and the correlative vision of a universe governed by universal law, cannot be paralleled, as yet, from anywhere outside Ionia. The earlier Hebrew prophets, and the Iranian prophet Zoroaster, may have had a vision of the nature of God as austere as that of Xenophanes, but their expression of it is enmeshed in the particular circumstances of themselves and their society. And because they lack such a vision, the cosmogonies of Babylonia, Canaan, or Egypt contain intelligent speculations and inferences, as well as the general notion of an established world-order, but are unable to free themselves definitely from the entrenched belief in the arbitrary power of an uncoordinated multiplicity of gods, and their world-systems evolve in a sequence of events without any internal necessity.

When this is granted, it may be readily admitted that on many great and small points of cosmogony and cosmology, the fact of borrowing is as certain as such things can be. One would expect the Milesians to have turned to the Near East as a source of ideas and of knowledge, and they did. But because they were borrowing for purposes of their own, they borrowed selectively and never wholesale. So Thales was stimulated by a cosmogony widespread in the Near East to see water as the origin of all and the support of the earth. Anaximander's Unbounded has been traced both to

Iranian and to Babylonian sources, and there may well be something in both conjectures. Certainly there are several other points
which point to Babylonian or Iranian influence on Anaximander,
and equally certainly the religious ideas of the Iranian peoples
will have had much to appeal to a Milesian thinker. Less certain
is the attempt to connect details of Milesian cosmogony with
those of the cosmogony attributed to 'Sanchuniathon' and other
Phoenician speculations. 'Sanchuniathon''s ideas are preserved
only in a later Greek translation, but they are alleged by the
Greek source to be of Phoenician origin and of great antiquity.
This claim has come to seem more and more reasonable as knowledge of the ancient Near East has increased. 'Sanchuniathon'
seems closer in spirit to the Milesians than any other Near Eastern
cosmology—perhaps it is significant that he is Phoenician. However this may be, in spite of the many points of possible contact,
there is no convincing proof that the cardinal ideas of Anaximander's system were anticipated inside or outside Greece, and
still more is this true of Anaximenes.

A special question is that of borrowings of mathematical and
astronomical knowledge from Babylonia and Egypt at this time,
by the Milesians or by other Greeks. The nature of the Babylonian
and Egyptian knowledge has been briefly indicated in the first
chapter. It would be in keeping with the general character of the
Milesians that they should take over and assimilate this knowledge
if it was available to them. Unfortunately the evidence for the
astronomical speculations of the Milesians, or of any sixth-century
Greeks, is sparse and difficult to handle. The subject remains
highly controversial, but it seems rather likely that some very
rudimentary astronomical (and mathematical) knowledge was
transmitted to Ionia at this time.

In connection with the question of Near Eastern influence, it is
right to mention what is known of other cosmogonies produced
by Greeks in the late seventh and early sixth centuries. The poet
Alcman, writing in Sparta not much if at all later than 600, incorporated in one of his choric songs a set of cosmogonical ideas in
which there are things suggestive both of the Milesians and of the

Near East. And in the sixth century Pherecydes of Syros composed a prose theogony which related in turn: the origin of the gods from three original gods who 'always existed'; the constructing of the rest of the world as it now is by one of those three, the creator-god Zas; and the final establishment of order by Zas after he had overcome a snaky monster representing the forces of confusion. These two examples show that, as is not surprising, interest in cosmogony was strong throughout the Greek world at this time, and they are good evidence of an openness to Near Eastern ideas. But it would be very misleading to class Pherecydes, and still more Alcman, with the Milesians as 'Presocratics'. For if the label 'Presocratic philosopher' has any point, it is that it marks off the Milesians and their successors as something new in the history of thought. Pherecydes and Alcman are, in this classification, on the same side as Hesiod and the ancient Near East. To put it more sharply, in the history of the human mind the Milesians are of cardinal importance, and Alcman and Pherecydes not at all. It has been the object of this chapter to explain where the difference lies.

CHAPTER THREE

Heraclitus

IN the middle of the sixth century, the Ionian cities of the Asiatic coast had for some time been tributaries of the kingdom of Lydia. The Lydian kings were not hard masters; the last of the line, Croesus, was distinctly phil-Hellene and was sincerely admired by many Greeks. But in 546 Croesus was defeated by the invading Persians under Cyrus, and the Ionians were faced with subjection to a new and much greater power. The new Persian empire was far more efficient and on a larger scale than anything these Greeks had yet seen. The Ionian territory would form an insignificant and peripheral part of the vast areas controlled by the Great King from the region of modern Iran.

Thales, according to Herodotus (1 170), had proposed that the Ionians should form themselves into a federal state to meet the Persian danger. This novel suggestion was not adopted, and the coastal cities were reduced to submission one by one. Many Ionians emigrated; the Persians seem to have interfered in the internal politics of the cities and to have checked the spread of political equality—or it was feared that they would do so. The citizens of Phocaea, a small Ionian city whose men were famous for expert seamanship, migrated in a body and after various adventures founded the city of Elea in southern Italy. The new city was to be famous for nothing but philosophy.

Ionia remained under the Persians for seventy years. During this time, only two Ionian thinkers are known to have been active who in any way carried further the ideas of the Milesians. One was Xenophanes of Colophon, whose theological utterances were used in the last chapter. But Xenophanes, a poet and a professional reciter of poetry who wandered about the Greek world, was not an original or systematic thinker. There is nothing to suggest that he tried to improve the Milesian framework where it seemed in danger of inconsistency. His own views were in certain crucial places vague and incoherent, if we may trust Aristotle, and in one fragment (fr. 34) he takes refuge in the thought that, after all, no man can know anything for certain. Still, Xenophanes is illuminating: he casts light, as has been seen, on the Milesians, and his difficulties and deficiencies cast light on the situation as it presented itself to the other Ionian thinker of this period, Heraclitus of Ephesus.

Heraclitus seems to have been born around 540 and to have lived past the turn of the century. Nothing suggests that he ever left his native town of Ephesus. His utterances suggest a striking and original personality in a partly self-willed intellectual isolation. In later centuries a great deal of biographical fabrication was called forth by the fact that Heraclitus was revered by the Stoics and had obviously been a remarkable man. Some of the stories invented about him are still occasionally repeated as true, but there is in fact hardly any reliable information about the life of Heraclitus beyond what little can be inferred from the fragments.

Of the actual words of Heraclitus there survive, cited by later writers, some eighty or ninety fragments, while there are many other passages in which his words are paraphrased or alluded to. The difficulty of interpreting his statements was already complained of by Aristotle and Theophrastus; Aristotle noted that they were frequently ambiguous, and Theophrastus remarked that Heraclitus sometimes left them incomplete, sometimes contradicted himself. Thereafter he was a byword for obscurity. So far as can be judged from our evidence, most of what he wrote consisted of isolated statements, terse and intentionally memorable prose sentences composed with great attention to rhythm and lacking for the most part any reference to a context. Lengthy explanations are avoided, and meaning is concealed in allusions, puns, portmanteau-words and ambiguities of construction. This style has often enough been compared to that of an oracle or a prophet. Yet it would be wrong to suppose that Heraclitus chooses obscurity entirely for its own sake, or for its effect on his audience. In many fragments, especially when denouncing the stupidity of ordinary people, Heraclitus speaks plainly enough; in some other cases, the fragments as cited may or must have been deprived of a context it originally had. In the only fragment in which Heraclitus offers a description of his own activity, he claims to-be 'defining each thing according to its nature, and showing how it is'. The fact seems to be that Heraclitus believed his style of utterance to be uniquely suitable to his subject-matter. If his utterances are like riddling oracles to most men, this is appropriate, since he believed, as will be explained, that the truth about things was like the meaning of an oracle, or the solution of a riddle, of which most men saw only the meaningless or misleading (perhaps deliberately misleading) exterior.

Heraclitus, in fact, seems to be the first exponent of an idea which has since been endemic in philosophy: that language must be used in a highly unusual way in order to fit the nature of things, which is conceived as being radically different from anything that is generally supposed. It is no mere accident that his style of thought and of expression is often reminiscent of Wittgenstein's *Tractatus Logico-Philosophicus,* and the resemblance goes even deeper than has been suggested. (Some ideas about the reasons for this resemblance will be offered at the end of this chapter.)

A careful and sympathetic examination of the fragments is the necessary beginning of any attempt at an interpretation of Heraclitus. Many of them can hardly be rendered adequately in English; nevertheless, English versions have been given here of all important fragments, as an inadequate English version is better than nothing. But it must always be remembered that such versions are only second-bests, and may already, in spite of the best intentions, incorporate wrong or unwarrantable assumptions about the meaning of Heraclitus.

It is characteristic of Heraclitus that his attitude to the fundamental assumptions of the Milesians is already highly critical.

Like the Milesians and Xenophanes, he believes that there is a single all-powerful deity in control of the universe; but on the questions arising from such a belief—the relation of the deity to what it controls, and the possibility of discovering the laws which it imposes—he takes up positions which appear to be subtler than those of his predecessors.

To begin with, the problem of knowledge. That men are easily deceived, that the scope of their knowledge is at best very limited, that their judgment is the creature of circumstances—these are themes of the earliest Greek literature. By contrast the Milesians must be assumed to have been highly optimistic about the possibility of true knowledge—an optimism which remained part of the Presocratic tradition. But Xenophanes introduces a deeper pessimism:

There is no man that has seen, nor any that will ever know, the exact truth concerning the gods and all the other subjects of which I speak. Even if a man should chance to speak the most complete truth, yet he himself does not know it; all things are wrapped in *appearances* (fr. 34).

The thought that reality is uniformly concealed from men by an impenetrable veil of 'seeming' (*dokos*) is quite new. It is natural to connect the appearance of this thought with the ideas of Anaximenes and Xenophanes on the unity of the universe. If God is all things, then appearances are certainly deceptive; and, though observation of the *kosmos* may yield generalisations and speculations about God's plans, true knowledge of them could only be had by a direct contact with God's mind. There are in this fragment the roots of various philosophical doubts which have often been advanced against scientific explanations.

Heraclitus agreed, as will be seen later, with Anaximenes and Xenophanes that the universe was a unity. Consequently, he necessarily agreed with them that reality was to some extent 'hidden':

The nature of things (*phusis*) is in the habit of concealing itself (fr. 123);

Latent structure is master of obvious structure (fr. 54).

But on the possibility of true knowledge for men his ideas were more complex and less totally pessimistic than those of Xenophanes, and they can be recovered from the fragments which spread themselves round this topic.

First, there are the remarks which associate knowledge with God, and emphasize the gulf between God and man:

It is characteristic of God, but not of man, to have discernment (fr. 78);

A man is considered silly by God (*or*: a god), as a child is by a man (fr. 79);

Of all whose words I have heard, none has reached so far as to know that the wise is different in nature from everything else (fr. 108);

One thing, that alone is wise, is unwilling and is willing to be called by the name 'Zeus' (fr. 32);

One thing is wisdom: to be skilled in the plan upon which all things are controlled throughout the universe (fr. 41).

The first two of these fragments are clearly expressed; it is important that they do not exclude all possibility of human knowledge. Men may, uncharacteristically, come to understanding, just as children can be educated. The next two fragments make wisdom the exclusive property of God, who as the underlying and controlling unity in the universe can be said to be 'different from everything else'. The name 'Zeus' is appropriate because Zeus is traditionally the strongest god, and his association with the thunderbolt was important for Heraclitus. There is also a characteristically Heraclitean reference to the verb *ʒēn* (to live) in the form of the word 'Zeus' used by Heraclitus here. He wishes to suggest that wisdom is the attribute of what is the only truly living thing. Such allusions depending on similarities between words are frequent in Heraclitus, for whom they contain important truths. (So too in fr. 79, the word used for 'god' is *daimon*, which can also be taken to mean 'he who knows'.) The name 'Zeus' is, on the other hand, inappropriate because of its traditional associations.

It may be that the 'wisdom' of which these fragments talk is to be distinguished from mere knowledge. The adjective *sophos* had, traditionally, practical connotations: a 'wise' man was one who could advise, act or perform well in some respect. The wording of the last fragment quoted above is unclear, and it is possible that it means that wisdom is knowing *how to control* the universe, not merely knowing how it is controlled.

However that may be, it is clear from other fragments that Heraclitus thought that some measure of true knowledge was attainable by men, and that he said something of how it was to be attained:

All that can be learnt of by seeing and hearing, this I value highest (fr. 55);

Men who love wisdom must be knowers of a great many things (fr. 35);

Much learning does not teach men understanding (fr. 40: part);

Bad witnesses to men are eyes and ears, when they belong to men whose souls cannot understand their language (fr. 107).

Here again Heraclitus takes up a position which is a refinement of that of the Milesians. He reaffirms the importance of first-hand inquiry, as in other places he attacked the dependence on the authority of tradition. But the results of such inquiry are not an end in themselves: it is necessary to have understanding (*noos*), in order to be able to interpret the evidence of eyes and ears. The step from the obvious to the latent truth is like the translation of utterances in a language which is foreign to most men. Heraclitus offers two other similes for this step. Fr. 56 says that men, in regard to knowledge of perceptible things, 'are the victims of illusion much as Homer was', and goes on to explain this remark by telling the story of how Homer was baffled by a riddle put to him. In fr. 93 he remarks, significantly:

The prince whose the oracle at Delphi is neither tells nor conceals: he gives a sign.

To reach the truth from the appearances, it is necessary to interpret, to guess the riddle, or divine the meaning of the oracle. But though this seems to be within the capacity of men, it is something most men never do. Heraclitus is very vehement in his attacks on the foolishness of ordinary men, and of what passes for knowledge among them. They are compared to sleepers in private worlds of their own (frr. 1, 2, 73); to children who believe what their parents tell them (fr. 74, cf. fr. 79); to dogs who bark at strangers (fr. 97); to deaf men, 'as good as not there' (fr. 34); to idiots who take fright at any sensible utterance (fr. 87). Their opinions are toys with which they childishly amuse themselves (fr. 70). The points made by these different similes are clear, but sometimes the remarks are even more explicit:

Most men do *not* have thoughts corresponding to what they encounter;* they do not know what they are taught, but imagine that they do (fr. 17);

Other men are unaware of what they are doing when awake, just as they are of what they forget about in sleep (fr. 1, part);

It is mere appearances that the most reliable of them keep hold of (fr. 28, part).

Together with these fragments go those which assail particular individuals by name. Heraclitus singled out for attack all those who had a wide reputation for knowledge or wisdom among his contemporaries: Homer, Hesiod, Archilochus, Hecataeus, Xenophanes, and Pythagoras (frr. 40, 42, 57, 129). It is perhaps significant that the Milesians were, so far as is known, spared, though there is implied criticism of many of their views in many fragments, and of Anaximander in particular in at least one. These wholesale denunciations are certainly suggestive of mania, not because they are so sweeping but because so much energy has clearly gone into the making of them. It must be remembered that Heraclitus is not writing to be read only, but to be heard and to resound in the memory.

If Heraclitus is to be so insistent on the lack of understanding shown by most men, it would seem only reasonable that he should offer further instructions for penetrating to the truth. The talk of riddle-guessing suggests that some kind of revelation, beyond human control, is necessary, and this is perhaps confirmed by another cryptic fragment:

* An allusion to some famous lines of Archilochus (fr. 68 Diehl[3]).

If one does not expect it, one will not find out the unexpected; it is not to be tracked down and no path leads to it (fr. 18).

Yet the application of this remark is uncertain. It must be left undecided how men achieve true insight, though the necessity of some revelation is plausible. The true wisdom, as has been seen, is closely associated with God, which suggests further that in advancing in wisdom a man becomes like, or part of, God. Some hints as to how this is done will be found later in the chapter.

If Heraclitus does not tell men how to achieve true wisdom, he does the next best thing. He communicates to them, in a suitably oracular style, the truths that his own insights have shown him. These truths are the content of what Heraclitus calls 'the *logos*'; '*logos*' is for him clearly a technical term in some fragments, but its meaning is not immediately obvious.

The word '*logos*', in ordinary Greek of this period, has a family of meanings: 'word', 'story', 'reckoning', 'proportion' are all possible renderings in different contexts, and all are relevant to its use by Heraclitus. The three fragments where it seems to be used as a technical term are as follows:

Of this *logos* which is so always men prove to have no understanding both before they have heard it and immediately on hearing it; though everything comes to be according to this *logos*, they are like persons who have no experience of it . . . (fr. 1, part);

Though the logos is common (*xunou*), most men live as if they had a private source of understanding (fr. 2);

Having heard not me, but the *logos*, it is wise to concur that all is one (fr. 50).

The last of these fragments shows that the *logos* is independent of what Heraclitus himself may have to say. The first suggests that it is the expression of the cosmic law; and this is borne out by a further fragment, which also sheds further light on what is meant by calling the *logos* 'common':

Those who speak with understanding (*xun noōi*) must make themselves strong with what is common (*xunōi*) to all, as a city does with

its law, and far more strongly than that. For all human laws are
nourished by the one divine law . . . (fr. 114, part).

The analogy here intended is that the law of a city makes it
strong because it stands above private interest; it is therefore
'common' to all both in the sense of 'impartial' and in the sense
that all alike share its benefit. In the same way, the *logos* is equally
true and equally accessible for all, and overrides private points of
view; as we should say, it is objective, not subjective. But the law
which the *logos* expresses, the 'divine law', is far more rigorous
and exceptionless than any human law, and therefore to 'speak
with understanding' involves being more carefully 'law-abiding'
than any good citizen.

The minimal sense that can well be given to the word *logos* here
is therefore something like: 'the true account of the law of the
universe'. But if that were all, it would be difficult to explain why
Heraclitus chooses to signify this by the single word *logos*. Given
his habits, it may be suspected that there are further layers of
meaning concealed in the word. A clue may be found in a development of meaning in *logos* around this time. In the first half of the
fifth century the sense of 'reason' or 'reasoning' appears to be well
established. This sense is presumably a development from the
meaning 'proportion', which is already attested in Heraclitus
(fr. 31). What is reasonable or unreasonable is in or out of proportion in some sense. Though there is no direct evidence, it is
likely that this development was already proceeding at the end of
the sixth century, and that Heraclitus is playing upon it here. If
this is correct, his thought is that the *logos* expresses a proportion
or analogy in the universe; and, therefore, that the *logos* is
reasonable and the law it expresses, in virtue of this proportion.
The reasonableness of the *logos* would further resolve a problem
to which Heraclitus does not directly offer a solution: what *public*
evidence of its own truth does the *logos* carry with it? It cannot be
a merely personal revelation.

All this remains unconfirmed speculation, unless it can be
shown that Heraclitus does indeed make appeals to proportions
and analogies in his account of the universe. In fact, some such

appeals have already been quoted: all similes can be seen as analogies, and there is a direct statement of proportion in fr. 79 (man : god :: child : man). In the rest of this chapter, it will become evident that the idea of analogy as a guide to the truth was indeed present in the mind of Heraclitus, and that the attempt to create analogies between words and things, sentences and states of affairs, is one of the principles of his extraordinary style. Above all, it is their value in providing analogies that explains the point of a large number of fragments in which Heraclitus describes various paradoxical states of affairs drawn from everyday experience. To these fragments we now turn.

Consider the following remarks:

Sea is purest and most unclean water: for fish, drinkable and life-giving; for men, undrinkable and deadly (fr. 61);
Of the bow the name is 'life', the work is death (fr. 48);*
A road is, upwards and downwards, one and the same (fr. 60);
Sickness it is that makes health pleasant and good, and so with hunger and satiety, weariness and rest (fr. 111).

These four fragments have been chosen to stand here because in them the actual words of Heraclitus are not in any doubt. They are representative of a whole group of fragments of which, as here, the point is drawn in a single way from ordinary experience. Each of the first three presents for consideration a single familiar subject, and then proceeds to show that within the unity of that subject there coexist opposites of some kind. The fourth is less typical in not giving an explicit unity, but instead demonstrating that the opposites named are dependent upon each other for their most essential qualities. Another important difference is that in the fourth fragment cited the opposites in question seem to be thought of as successive, not as coexistent.

It is necessary to remember that to look at these fragments in an abstract way is to impose upon them a pattern that may be misleading. Heraclitus had no abstract vocabulary at his command. At least one of the fragments presented, the 'road', can be read as

---

* The word *bios* could mean either 'life' or 'bow'.

asserting, not the coexistence of opposites in a single subject, but
the *identity* of opposites. 'The road up' is the opposite of 'the road
down': yet they are identical. Other fragments make it clear that
Heraclitus did indeed wish to say that certain opposites were not
merely coexistent or mutually interdependent, but identical with
one another:

> [Hesiod] did not know what day and night are; they are one (fr. 57);
> The same thing is in us as the living and the dead, the awake and
> the sleeping, the young and the old; these change to become those, and
> those change back again to become these (fr. 88).

Here the identity of certain opposites is deduced from the fact
that they change into one another, which is a strong form of
mutual interdependence. If the ideas of Anaximenes and Xenophanes are recalled, it is clear what is Heraclitus' motive, at least in
part, for these unifications. He is concerned, as would be expected,
to work out a way in which the universe can be a true unity,
while leaving room for the diversity of the perceptible world.
Here again he picks up the problems that we find in Xenophanes
and tries to work out a better solution. Xenophanes 'gave no
clear account', according to Aristotle; 'he simply surveys the
whole world and says that the one is God' (*Metaphysics* 986ᵇ
21–5).

These fragments, then, are Heraclitus' analogies, drawn from
experience, and aimed at demonstrating the unity, in general, of
pairs of opposites. To this end, he collects examples which show
opposites inextricably bound up together with each other in
various ways. These examples, it is clear, took up a considerable
part of his book, and have always attracted, as they were meant
to, a great deal of interest. Historically, they are interesting as the
first deliberately sought philosophical 'examples', and as the
forerunners of the collections of puzzles which were made in the
late fifth century for 'sophistic' purposes, and which served as
raw material on which, in the fourth century, the creators of
logic tested and refined the instruments they had devised. Some
of them continue to be relevant to philosophical discussion, and

they have stimulated, and continue to stimulate, many imaginations not concerned with philosophy or with cosmology.

From these illustrations of unity in opposites, the path back to the *logos* that tells us that 'all things are one' runs through two remarkable fragments in which Heraclitus is visibly attempting a generalisation from all the particular situations. Of men, in general, he complains:

> They do not understand how what is at variance is in agreement with itself: a *back-turning structure* (*palintropos harmoniē*) like that of the bow and of the lyre (fr. 51).

The first part of this statement seems clear. Men fail to understand the general truth illustrated by the 'paradoxes', that what is at variance (from itself) is in agreement with itself. The words translated by 'is at variance' and 'is in agreement' have the primary meaning of 'is drawn apart' and 'is drawn together', and therefore suggest some kind of alternating movement.

In the second part, Heraclitus goes on to give a further description of the general situation he has in mind, and the interpretation of these words has been much debated. The word *harmoniē*, which here and in fr. 54 has been translated by 'structure', is a noun derived from the verb *harmozein*, 'to fit together'. The noun appears in Homer with reference to concrete 'fittings together', such as those of carpentry or masonry, but also in another sense, that of 'treaty' or 'covenant'; the verb shows a similar range of meaning in early Greek. The basic notion seems to be that of the mutual adjustment of two or more different components to form a structure which is more than the mere sum of its parts. This basic meaning was still alive in the late sixth century, for it is about this time that it gives off a subsidiary special meaning, that of a 'mode' in music. The thought behind this derivation seems to be that, in tuning his lyre in a certain way, the musician is mutually adjusting the strings so that the notes playable form a particular system of pitch-relationships. Heraclitus, it is reasonable to assume, uses *harmoniē* in its widest sense. The translation 'structure' tries to render this breadth of meaning,* but fails to capture completely the notion of 'mutual adjustment'. The ways in which the word *harmoniē* might naturally be applied to a bow and to a lyre are fairly clear. Applied to a bow, it might refer simply to the structure of the arms of the bow, if that were complex, as it was in the composite bow; or to the structure of the strung bow which the arms and the string were mutually adjusted. The second way of taking it is clearly preferable since it applies to all kinds of bow and since the string and the arms pull different ways when the bow is at rest and move different ways when it is drawn, so that they are an apt picture of a marriage of opposites. Applied to a lyre, *harmoniē* might refer to the structure of the unstrung lyre, or to that of the strung lyre whether tuned or not, or to that of the lyre tuned in a particular mode. Here it is not immediately clear what the opposites are which are unified.

To choose between these possibilities, and to grasp the full point of the double simile, it is necessary to understand the adjective which Heraclitus chooses to qualify *harmoniē*. The witnesses to this fragment are divided between *palintropos* and *palintonos*. In either of these the prefix *palin-* must be taken to mean 'back', 'in a contrary direction'; but *-tropos* represents the notion of turning, and so of a movement which alters, while *-tonos* represents the notion of stretching or tension and seems to refer to a static situation. *Palintropos* is the better attested here directly and indirectly, and Parmenides uses the word *palintropos* with emphasis in a passage (DK 28 B 6) which may well allude to Heraclitus. But these external considerations are not quite strong enough to be decisive by themselves. Considerations of sense come into play, and these make the choice between the two adjectives part of a wider debate about the form of Heraclitus' thought.

If *palintonos* is correct, then the bow and lyre are thought of as not functioning, but at rest and in a state of tension, as indeed

---

* For the evolution of the meaning of 'structure', see the *Oxford English Dictionary*.

they both are when strung. If this is so, then the unity of opposites expresses itself most typically in a static state, an equilibrium in which the opposed forces balance each other.

If *palintropos* is correct, then the bow and the lyre are thought of as in use. Their proper functioning implies the movement in opposite or alternate directions of their complicated structure. This is easy to explain of the bow. To apply it to the lyre, it seems best to take into account the special musical meaning of *harmoniē*, and to take the movements in opposite directions as the alterations in pitch as the melody ascends and descends. If this is right, the unity of opposites expresses itself most typically in alternating movements in opposite directions.

These two opposed interpretations may be labelled for convenience the 'tension' and the 'oscillation' interpretations of Heraclitus. They both seem to go back to the fourth century at least. This is not the place to decide finally between them. (It may be added that the musical interpretation of *palintropos harmoniē*, as applied to the lyre, is supported by some further evidence (DK 22 A 22).)

In whichever way it is to be understood, it is clear at least that fr. 51 lies at the core of Heraclitus' thought. A generalised truth about the unity of opposites is expressed by taking the word *harmoniē*, capable of a wide range of meaning, in its greatest generality and propping it up, as it were, by the similes of the bow and the lyre. In another fragment there is an equally remarkable attempt to generalise along the same lines:

'Conjunctions: wholes and not wholes, the converging the diverging, the consonant the dissonant, from all things one, and from one all things (fr. 10).

It is doubtful what exactly the word translated here by 'conjunctions' was; there is a choice between two readings, but in either case the significance of the word is close to that of *harmoniē*. The 'conjunctions' are the particular instances of the general situation described in fr. 51 The point of fr. 10 seems to be that in making a general statement about all these instances, it itself

furnishes a further instance. The pattern of fr. 10 is that of the
typical 'paradox' fragment, exemplified in frs. 60 and 61. As we
might put it, the concept of a 'conjunction' is itself a 'conjunction'.

The two fragments that have just been considered lie at the
core of Heraclitus' thought. His doctrines on the nature of God
and of the observable world, and their interrelations, can be seen
as applications of fr. 51. It is this fact that gives unity to his
teachings and substance to his claim (implicit in fr. 1) to be following the *logos* in everything he says.

It was suggested in the last chapter how a new theology
initiated a new kind of cosmology, and how fundamental difficulties must quickly have shown themselves. In general, it
might be asked of a Milesian thinker whether God was or was not
everything. If he is, then there is the problem of explaining the
diversity, transience and apparent imperfection and self-contradiction of a great deal of the observable world. But if not, then
there is the problem of the relations between God and the rest of
the universe, and the nature and mechanism of the control
exercised by the one over the other. Anaximander can hardly
have provided any precise thought on these questions; Anaximenes and Xenophanes both seem to have attempted a radically
unifying solution without, perhaps, becoming aware of the full
depth of the problem.

Heraclitus has already been seen to be a 'unifier', and to have
rested his claims upon the application of the *logos*. The most
explicit application of the doctrine of the *harmoniē* to the universe
as a whole is the following:

God is day night, winter summer, war peace, surfeit famine; but he
is modified (*alloioutai*), just as fire, when incense is added to it, takes its
name from the particular scent of each different spice (fr. 67).

The important pairs of contraries 'day-night' and 'winter-
summer' are unified by being different aspects of God, so that
God is, at least, that which provides the unity through time of
certain large-scale cosmic alternations. There is some reason to

think that 'war-peace' and 'surfeit-famine' are Heraclitean names for other large-scale cosmic oscillations. So the unity of the universe will consist, essentially, in the fact that all the large-scale cosmic processes are oscillations in the state of God. Just so a fire on an altar may persist; yet according as different incense is thrown on to it, it gives off a different scent, by which, at each different time, it can be identified. Because the incense is something so inessential to the fire, this simile suggests, far more than that of the bow or the lyre, the existence of a gap between the superficial appearances and the hidden unity.

Fr. 67 shows that for Heraclitus theology and physics are one. But God is not simply, as this fragment might suggest, a lawlike self-regulating mechanism. It was not natural to Greek thinkers of any period to suppose that what was self-moving and lawlike in behaviour was dead or mindless. As for the Milesians and Xenophanes, so for Heraclitus too God is of necessity something pre-eminently living and intelligent. Xenophanes as usual is instructive: he announces of his God that

without effort, he agitates all things by the thought of his mind (fr. 25)

and that he is

not like mortal men in his bodily form, nor in his thought (fr. 23).

The evidence that Heraclitus' God has a mind has already been presented. It consists of frr. 32, 41 and 108, which attribute wisdom to God, as the only being that knows the plan upon which all things are governed. So the mind of God thinks the plan upon which God acts, and as with Xenophanes there is presumably no hiatus between thought and action. It is natural to identify the plan, the *gnomē* of fr. 41, with the 'divine law' of fr. 114, which has also been quoted already.

If God has a mind, clearly further problems arise. It is natural to ask where this mind is situated, and what marks it off from the rest of the contents of the universe. 'Hidden' as it is, it cannot transcend space and time. Anaximander and Anaximenes had done their best in this direction, by placing 'the Divine' beyond human reach in space and depriving it of ordinary physical properties. But for Heraclitus God is everywhere, in the continual changes of the world-order. In what form? Heraclitus seems to have answered: as *fire*.

That God is a fiery mind is suggested indirectly by the connection of human souls, in their wisest state, with fire (the evidence will be given later), and directly by the evidence which assigns to fire a central and controlling place in the universe:

Thunderbolt steers all things (fr. 64);

This world-order (*kosmos*) was made neither by god nor by man, but it was always and is and shall be; fire ever-living, being kindled by measures and being quenched by measures (fr. 30).

To which two fragments may be appended the Aristotelian interpretation of Heraclitus, in which fire is the material cause of everything.

It is still not clear in exactly what way the equations: '*kosmos* = fire' and 'fire = mind of God' are to be interpreted. Before these questions are further treated, it will be convenient to discuss the 'external' aspect of God, in other words the observable world-order. To this fr. 30 makes a natural transition.

The doctrine of the *palintropos harmoniē* had interesting repercussions on the general scheme of cosmology. The controlling divinity being no longer spatially separate from the world-order, there was no longer any argument for the plurality of the *kosmoi*, or for the bounding of the one *kosmos* in space or in time. Fr. 30 sums up some of this; for the fact that the *kosmos* was not limited spatially there is only an argument from silence.

The *kosmos* was still the scene of a constant struggle between opposed forces, as in Anaximander. But the struggle was not, as in Anaximander, something beyond the plan of God, and which the divine justice had to step in and regulate. Heraclitus says, with an emphasis clearly directed against Anaximander:

But one must know that war is universal (*xunon*), and that justice *is* strife, and that all things happen according to strife and necessity (fr. 80).

In other words, the perpetual struggle of opposites and the justice that balances them are indistinguishable and both equally present in every event, which occurs as a necessary part of the divine plan. Every event, then, can be analysed into encroachments (in a sense yet to be explicated) of one opposite on another —acts of 'war' or 'strife'. Hence:

War is father of all, and king of all . . . (fr. 53, part).

But every such encroachment is also 'justice' because it is laid down by the divine law as part of a regular plan. This does not necessarily mean that the scores between the pairs of opposites are always evened up instantaneously, though it is clear that the plan involves the preservation, in general, of certain 'measures', those mentioned in fr. 30. In one fragment an explicit assurance is given that the divine justice will preserve the cosmic order:

Sun will not overstep his measures; for the Erinyes, the assistants of Justice, will find him out (fr. 94).

where the Erinyes are strife (*eris*) personified. And the inextricable combination of 'strife' between two opposites and 'justice' as a set of rules is illuminated in one further striking image:

Time (*aiōn*) is a child at play, playing draughts; a child's is the kingdom (fr. 52).

Here, as probably in Anaximander, 'Time' is a name for God, with an etymological suggestion of his eternity. The infinitely old divinity is a child playing a board game as he moves the cosmic pieces in combat according to rule.

On the analogy of the bow and the lyre, it is no surprise that the order and unity of the *kosmos* should depend upon the existence of opposed forces. But, as was shown in discussing fr. 51, it is possible to be uncertain whether Heraclitus was there thinking of a tension between opposites, or an oscillation between them, or both. It was argued in favour of oscillation that the *palintropos harmoniē* is best interpreted as something permanent which is expressed in the way bow and lyre function by alternations in time—the arms of the bow are drawn back and together, but then spring forwards and apart, and the high and low notes of the lyre alternate when it is played. The same alternatives appear in the interpretation of Heraclitus' physical system. With a 'tension' interpretation, the struggle between the opposites will always be evenly balanced, gains in one region by one force being always *simultaneously* offset by equal gains elsewhere by the opposed force. With an 'oscillation' interpretation, the struggle may go everywhere in favour of either opposite, but alternately, the alternation being subject to a law determining the periods during which each prevails.

It should be clear that the similes of bow and lyre already favour the 'oscillation' interpretation for the cosmology, since when bow and lyre function there is oscillation in time. Nor does it count against this that Plato in a well-known passage (*Sophist* 242D-243A) contrasts Heraclitean tension with Empedoclean oscillation. Plato's concern here is ontology, not cosmology; he is concerned with ultimate reality, not with appearances. Most of the other evidence points in the same direction. Thus, fr. 67, already cited, mentions God as the unity behind at least two pairs of opposites which are expressed by oscillations, namely, day-night and winter-summer, and (if the report of Theophrastus is reliable) war-peace and famine-surfeit were also names for longer periods of cosmic oscillation (DK 22 A 1, B 65). And the best of our later witnesses, Aristotle (esp. *de Caelo* 279ᵇ 14–17 and 280ᵃ 11–19) and Theophrastus, agree in ascribing to Heraclitus an 'oscillation' theory of cosmic processes. Against all this, there is no single piece of clearly good evidence for a 'tension' cosmology. Two fragments about paradoxical states of affairs—the 'river' (fr. 12) and the 'barley-drink' (fr. 125) would qualify, if there was anything to show that they were meant as similes with direct reference to cosmology; these will be treated separately later.

In fr. 30 the *kosmos* is described as 'fire ever-living, being kindled by measures and being quenched by measures'. The relation between fire and other constituents of the kosmos is further treated:

For fire all things are exchanged, and fire for all things, as for gold goods and for goods gold (fr. 90);

The turnings (*tropai*) of fire: first sea, and of sea half earth, half *prēstēr* . . . (the earth?) is dissolved to become sea, and is measured in the same proportion as was before (fr. 31).

All three fragments have this in common, that they stress the lawlikeness of the cosmic processes. When fire is 'kindled' or 'quenched', which is when it is 'received' or 'given' in exchange for other things, measures are observed which are like the standard rates of exchange relating gold to goods of all kinds. Gold, being universally acceptable, provides a medium of exchange and a measure of value: so too fire in the *kosmos*. The details of fr. 31 are obscure, but here too a 'proportion' is preserved; presumably, as much sea is derived back from the earth as was absorbed in creating earth previously. It is, then, at least clear that in Heraclitean cosmology the components turn into one another according to certain rules which keep certain quantities constant.

The mechanism of change is slightly illuminated by evidence from Aristotle:

Some say that everything is in a state of becoming and flux, and that nothing has any firm existence, with the sole exception of one persisting thing beneath the changes, from which, by rearrangement, everything naturally comes to be; this seems to be the meaning of Heraclitus of Ephesus among many others (*de Caelo* 298^b 29–33);

Some [Heraclitus must be meant here] say nothing about the shape [of fire] but simply make it the thing of which the parts are finest, and then they say that other things are produced by the putting together of fire, as when gold dust is solidified in the furnace (*de Caelo* 304^a 18–21).

The simile of the furnace is a reminder that metallurgy and cooking were the main sources of empirical data for any Greek interested in the transformations of material things. In both, fire is the main agent of change, and the proportions of ingredients are important for the nature of the final product.

Any further reconstruction of the system of physical changes in Heraclitus is necessarily conjecture. A natural starting-point is the report by Theophrastus, preserved by Diogenes Laertius (IX 8–11, in DK 22 A 1) according to which the four main constituents, fire, air, water, earth, were related by a system of changes as follows:

$$\text{Fire} \rightleftharpoons \text{Air} \rightleftharpoons \text{Water} \rightleftharpoons \text{Earth.}$$

Yet even in Theophrastus' report there are signs that this cannot have been the whole story. The reconstruction that will now be offered is based only upon plausibilities, but it seems to fit well with most of the evidence.

Two important pairs of opposites are singled out in:

Cold things grow warm, warm grows cold, wet grows dry, and parched grows moist (fr. 126).

From this it is reasonable to infer that the interchanges cold-hot, hot-cold, wet-dry, dry-wet, were of particular importance for Heraclitus. A coherent scheme can be constructed on the assumption that all change is to be accounted for in terms of these four changes. In order to construct this scheme, it is necessary to identify earth, water, air, and some fourth thing with the combinations cold + dry, cold + wet, hot + wet, and hot + dry respectively. This identification is part of the Aristotelian theory of the physical world, but there is no reason why it should not have been invented previously; indeed, it would suggest itself immediately the two pairs of opposites had been taken to be important. For Aristotle, the combination hot + dry is identified with fire; but for Heraclitus it must not be assumed that 'fire' in this sense is equivalent to the divine fire. There will then be eight possible changes between the four components, instead of six as in Theophrastus' report:

$$
\begin{array}{ccc}
\text{Air} & \rightleftharpoons & \text{Fire} \\
= \text{hot} + \text{wet} & & = \text{hot} + \text{dry} \\
\Updownarrow & & \Updownarrow \\
\text{Water} & \rightleftharpoons & \text{Earth} \\
= \text{cold} + \text{wet} & & = \text{cold} + \text{dry}
\end{array}
$$

From fr. 31 it appears that *prēstēr* must be a name for the hot and wet component named 'air' in the diagram. This agrees well with the possible etymologies of the word, which would connect it for Heraclitus with two verbs meaning 'burn' and 'blow'; its normal usage in Greek is to denote a waterspout or hurricane attended by lightning. All this makes it an excellent word to use for a hot atmospheric component of the *kosmos*.

If this is right, fr. 31 mentions the changes water-earth, water-air, and earth-water. Further, Theophrastus reports that Heraclitus spoke of two 'exhalations', one, which was dark and moist, from the sea, and one, bright and dry, from the earth. Again, the doctrine of two exhalations appears in Aristotle's own physical system, but again there is no reason why it should not have been inspired by Heraclitus, and Heraclitus' strange theory of the sun, also reported by Theophrastus, depends essentially on the two exhalations. These will then correspond to the changes water-air and earth-fire. All the other changes required by this reconstruction are attested by Theophrastus except for fire-earth. Many of them, it is clear, can be connected with facts of common observation.

Whether or not this reconstruction of the system of physical changes is correct, it remains to ask what patterns these changes make in time, locally and in the *kosmos* as a whole. It has already been argued that the *kosmos* as a whole oscillated between two extremes, and the evidence for this view has been briefly described. From some rather late authorities (in DK 22 A 13) it seems likely that the oscillation had a period of 10,800 or 12,000 years. At one extreme, the whole *kosmos* will be 'fire', and at the other it will be water. It appears that Heraclitus used the terms 'war' and 'famine' for the oscillation from 'fire' to water and 'peace' and 'satiety' for that from water to 'fire'.

Our sources of information make no distinction between the hot, dry component that has been labelled 'fire', and the cosmic fire which is associated with God, underlies all changes, and is more like a process or agent of change than a component. In the absence of explicit statements by Heraclitus, it must be assumed that the relation between these two was left unclear, unless indeed the very existence of a hot, dry component is denied. This difficulty is not an isolated one, but goes to the heart of Heraclitus' system and there links up with difficulties derived from other directions. It is worth noticing, in any case, the conceptual ambiguity of 'fire', which in Greek as in English, may easily be thought of both as a component of the world and as an agent or process of change.

Water, too, is closely associated with change in the famous words so often attributed to Heraclitus: 'all is in flux' (*panta rhei*). The origin of this attribution is an undoubtedly genuine statement by Heraclitus about the paradoxical properties of rivers:

> Upon those who step into the same rivers, there flow different waters in different cases (fr. 12).

The wording leaves it open whether the 'different cases' are produced by stepping in at different times or at different places or both. The remark is subtler when it refers to different times, for then it points to the fact not merely that a river contains many different pieces of water, but that the very being of a river depends upon its changing its waters constantly through time. If it did not flow, it would be no river. In other words, it has to change constantly in order to stay the same *river*. The same idea is conveyed in another image:

> The barley-drink (*kukeōn*) comes apart if not stirred (fr. 125)

for the barley-drink is made by stirring up wine, honey and barley-grains together, and these components will settle into separate layers unless the drink is kept in motion. The *kukeōn* has to move in order to stay as it is.

Both the river and the barley-drink are subtle examples of the *palintropos harmoniē*. But there is nothing in them to suggest that either of them had any direct application to the system of physical changes. Yet Plato and Aristotle believed that this application was made by Heraclitus, and their testimony (Plato, *Cratylus*

402A; Aristotle *Metaphysics* 1010ᵃ 10–15) cannot simply be dismissed. It can, however, be shown to be less convincing by the observation that both Plato and Aristotle know the river fragment in a version which can hardly be Heraclitean, and which is closely associated with the late fifth-century self-styled 'follower' of Heraclitus, the philosopher Cratylus. The suspect version states: 'You could not step twice into the same river.' To deny in this way the existence of a unity persisting through change is not Heraclitean, but it is very characteristic of Cratylus. Aristotle relates of Cratylus the anecdote that he 'rebuked Heraclitus for saying that you could not step twice into the same river; he (Cratylus) thought you could not even do so *once*.' Whether or not this anecdote is true, it is known that Cratylus was concerned to deny that any kind of persisting object was to be found in the perceptible world, and that he called himself a 'Heraclitean'. It seems therefore almost certain that the second version of the 'river', and the 'flux doctrine', are 'interpretations' of Heraclitus due to Cratylus. Heraclitus no doubt held that change was incessantly occurring, even in the most stable objects, as indeed fr. 126 suggests; but this is not the same as the 'flux doctrine' according to which the components of every object change completely from moment to moment.

There is little information about any further details in the cosmology of Heraclitus. In particular, nothing is known of any explanation of the movements of the heavenly bodies, except for those of the sun. Of the sun the report of Theophrastus tells that it originates, 'new every day', as a bowl-shaped object in which some hot exhalation from the earth is trapped. As a result the bowl and its contents begin to ascend, and the heat from the bowl acts upon the earth and draws up to itself further fiery exhalation, so that the sun rises steadily and becomes progressively hotter. By degrees the effect upon the sea begins to outweigh that upon the earth, so that the exhalations rising are more moist than dry, with the result that the fire receives less and less nourishment and from noon declines to its final extinction. This process repeats itself every day, a different bowl being needed for each day. Eclipses, and the seasonal variations of the sun's movement, were explained using this model. Of the origin and location of the bowls nothing is reported. The stars, too, are bowls full of ignited substances.

This strange theory allows the inference that all fire had a tendency to move upwards, or at least outwards from the centre of the *kosmos*, and hence that earth had a tendency to move inwards. This further suggests that there is a region beyond that of the stars where fire collects if not hindered. But all further treatment of the general arrangement of the *kosmos* is hindered by an almost complete lack of evidence, and it is probable that Heraclitus was not at all explicit.

If the cosmology of Heraclitus was impressionistic, his doctrines concerning sleep and waking, life and death, and the nature and fate of the souls of men seem to be deliberately mysterious. It has been shown that Anaximenes probably, and possibly the other Milesians, made an analogy between the role of God in the world and that of the soul in the body, with the suggestion that individual souls are detached pieces of the divine stuff, and may perhaps rejoin it after death. The same analogy seems to be implicit in Heraclitus. At least it is clear that the soul is responsible for moving and controlling the body and for intelligence, and that it is best when dry:

> When a man is drunk, he is led by a young child and stumbles as he goes, unaware of where he is going; for his soul is moist (fr. 117);
> Dry soul is wisest and best (fr. 118).

Other pieces of evidence confirm that the soul in its best state is fiery. Aristotle reports (*de Anima* 405ᵃ 25–6) that Heraclitus says that the soul is 'the exhalation from which he constructs everything else', a mysterious phrase but one which is consistent with the soul being a kind of fire. Another obscurely worded fragment, fr. 26, seems to suggest, like some early Hindu texts, that sleep is a retreat for the soul's fire into an inner citadel, the outer 'fires' accounting for sense-perception being quenched.

Similarly, fragments (frr. 24, 25, 63) apparently relating to the fate of the soul after death can most easily be accounted for by taking that fate to have been decided by the condition in which the soul was at death. A good and wise soul, being fiery, would at departure ascend to the upper regions, whether it was absorbed into the divine fire or, as some evidence suggests, became a star (DK 22 A 15). A less good soul would find difficulty in ascending, because an admixture of cold and moisture would drag it down; the strange myth in Plutarch's dialogue 'On the Face which is Seen in the Orb of the Moon', according to which most souls undergo a kind of purgatory in the dark region between the earth and the moon, may possibly preserve some of Heraclitus' ideas.

Two further fragments relating to souls look important but are difficult to interpret:

The limits of soul you would not find out by going about, though you travelled every road; so deep a *logos* does it have (fr. 45);
To the soul belongs a *logos* that increases itself (fr. 115).

'The *logos* of soul' may be expected to be the true account of its nature. A 'deep *logos*' is one that is profound and subtle—the metaphor is common in early Greek. That the soul has a deep *logos* will then explain why its limits (*peirata*) are not to be found, which is to say that it cannot be characterised or defined. No investigation will produce a complete account of soul, which therefore must be of unlimited complexity. The same conclusion is suggested by fr. 115; if the *logos* of soul 'increases itself' it presumably grows greater without limit. These fragments seem then to have a mutual coherence, even if the self-increasing complexity of soul is not explained.

A further explanation may be offered which would take these fragments to reflect Heraclitus' awareness of a central difficulty in his system of ideas. First, it will be seen that the doctrine about souls offers some justification for the hypothesis suggested earlier that men can make progress in wisdom just in so far as they make themselves divine; they can do this because their souls are potentially divine and can realise their potentiality. This completes a cycle of associations, wisdom—God—fire—soul—wisdom, which must have been intended by Heraclitus. Now in connection with each member of the cycle an analogous problem presents itself; each has been noticed separately in the course of this chapter. Each member of the cycle is distinct from, and transcends in some way, the ordinary world in which it nevertheless seems to be entangled. 'Wisdom', or 'the wise', is 'distinct from everything'; yet some men are wise, and the wise God is everything else too. God *is* the *kosmos*, but is also beyond or beneath the *kosmos*. Fire is one of the physical components of the *kosmos*, but is also the agent or process or mind that controls the changes of such components. Soul is subject to physical transformation, yet is also the controller and agent of such transformation. In view of the cycle of associations, Heraclitus must have recognised all these problems as one problem, if he recognised them at all.

The evidence that Heraclitus *did* recognise this problem, apart from general considerations about his intelligence and intellectual honesty, consists only of fr. 115 and fr. 10. Both of these suggest, without being forced unduly, that Heraclitus was aware of an infinite regress made necessary by his thought. Fr. 10 shows that the most general description of the 'unity-in-opposites' is at the same time an *example* of that same kind of thing; so that a *logos* containing fr. 10 will be referring to itself among other things. In the same way, a *logos* in the mind of God or man which gives an account of that mind will have to refer to itself. Once this is admitted, we have the familiar 'map' paradox: a map of an area which includes the map itself will have, if true in all details, to contain an infinite procession of maps: a map of itself, a map of the map of itself, and so *ad infinitum*.

Now, the only plausible way to detach God from the *kosmos*, for Heraclitus, is to think of God's mind as a perfect map of the *kosmos*, which is itself in the *kosmos* but not identical with it. In this way the central problem of Heraclitus' thought can be seen to issue in the 'self-mapping' paradox suggested by frr. 10 and

115. It may still, reasonably, be objected that this is a construction without sufficient basis in the texts. But it can hardly be denied that Heraclitus takes his God to have in his mind something like a 'plan' for the running of the universe, which is perfectly carried out; which is the equivalent of a perfect map of the universe. This way of seeing the central difficulties of Heraclitus can also help to explain the similarity in tone and approach between Heraclitus and the early Wittgenstein. Alphabetic writing, which pictured speech by arranging characters in an order, and the development at the same time of explicitly formulated general laws, must have helped the growth of the idea that all reality could be represented in language, and conversely that all language not representing reality was false or nonsensical. As the early Wittgenstein, inspired by the new 'language' of formal logic, tried to mark out the limits of significant language-use as that which depicts the world, and thereby to exhibit some truths about the structure of reality reflected in the true structure of language, and to demolish as meaningless all metaphysics, so Heraclitus seems to be using his new consciousness of sentences as formulae for exhibiting reality, suggested by his use of the term *logos*, to exhibit the structure of things in appropriately constructed language. In part of fr. 1 he describes himself as 'delimiting each thing according to its nature and declaring (*phrazōn*) how it is'. The devices he uses are not those of formal logic, but etymologies, puns, antitheses and portmanteau-words. He attacks the foolishness of ordinary men, as Wittgenstein attacks metaphysics. Both philosophers, being dominated by an ideal of how language should be used, are systematic in thought but discrete in expression. Both try to expel mystery and end with a central difficulty that leaves things more mysterious than before.

CHAPTER FOUR

Pythagoras and the Greek West

'THE Greek West' is a convenient name for what came to be called in antiquity 'Great Greece' (*Magna Graecia*): the area of Greek settlement in the Western Mediterranean, above all in Sicily and southern Italy. Most of the Greek cities there had been founded in the last half of the seventh century, but they received fresh waves of emigrants from old Greece throughout the sixth, especially from Ionia after the Persian conquest.

These young and often very prosperous Greek cities in the West were to the older Greek world at this time something of what America was to Europe in the nineteenth century A.D., an underdeveloped region offering the prospect of new opportunities and wealth. The Greek settlers dispossessed or treated with the native tribes and acquired large tracts of rich agricultural land. Some of the new cities were also well placed to be markets and entrepôts for some of the most lucrative trade in the Mediterranean. The wealth amassed was conspicuously consumed, as may still be seen from the ruins of Acragas and Selinus in Sicily, with their extravagant use of space and their great temples, enormous by the standards of old Greece. On the Italian mainland, the city of Sybaris became a byword for luxury before it was destroyed, about 510, by its neighbour and rival, Croton.

Culturally, the West was probably still rather provincial at the end of the sixth century. In the visual arts, at least, there seems to be a dependence on the Greek mainland. In literature, there had early been one great name, Stesichorus of Himera, but towards 500 we hear only of two citizens of Rhegium in Italy: Theagenes, who produced allegorical interpretations of Homer in

which the various gods were taken to represent such constituents
of the world as appeared in Milesian-style cosmologies; and
Ibycus, a graceful lyric poet, whose fragments reveal some interest
in cosmology and astronomy. The leading personage of this
chapter, Pythagoras, was not born in Great Greece; he arrived
there as a migrant from his native island of Samos.

Around the figure of Pythagoras there very soon grew up a
great mass of legend. Even towards the end of the fifth century,
when history begins to be written in earnest, there was probably
rather little surviving in the way of reliable information about the
facts of his life, his teachings, and the activities of his sect or
school in the cities of Great Greece. The school itself had ceased
to exist, its political activities having made it so unpopular that it
was broken up, and its members killed or exiled, around 450.
While it had existed its members had been bound not to reveal,
or even commit to writing, the doctrines of their master. Even of
the political activities themselves there was little public record. In
the absence of reliable information, real or pretended Pythagoreans repeatedly fostered exaggerated and miraculous accounts.
Such was the magic of the name of Pythagoras in later centuries
that there repeatedly appeared persons who wished to be regarded
as his followers and labelled themselves 'Pythagoreans'. Such
people would project their own ideas back upon their hero, so
adding to the mass of misinformation.

For these reasons, the study of Pythagoras involves the close
examination of the various sources of information, and accounts
of his activity will vary widely according to the value placed on
each by different scholars. There is no space in this book for a
a discussion of the sources. The account of Pythagoras that follows
will in general assume that the only testimony that can be admitted
as *prima facie* trustworthy is that of authors earlier than the mid-
fourth century, together with that of the teachings known as the
'Pythagorean *akousmata*' of which our knowledge derives from
a work by Aristotle which is now lost. In the mid-fourth century
there begin debates about the true nature of Pythagoras' teaching

and new 'interpretations' are offered which have greatly confused all the subsequent tradition. The principles just enunciated mean that a generally sceptical attitude will be taken towards all those sources which purport to give precise and detailed accounts of Pythagoras' doctrines, which in turn means that the contribution of Pythagoras and his earliest disciples to the intellectual life of their time cannot be determined with any certainty. Disappointing as this conclusion is, it is the only justifiable one, and was very likely that of Aristotle.

Some outward facts in Pythagoras' life can be given with fair certainty. He was born on Samos before the middle of the sixth century, the son of a gem-engraver. He acquired a reputation in Ionia as a polymath, and eventually migrated to Croton in Italy. The date of this migration cannot well be later than 520, and the most likely occasion for it is given by the political turmoils in Samos in the years after 525. In Croton Pythagoras founded a society the like of which had not been seen before in Greece. Political clubs, whose members helped one another to obtain office, and generally acted as a *bloc* in politics, were probably already common, as they certainly were in fifth-century Athens. But the Pythagoreans, though they too acquired by their solidarity and their beliefs great political strength, were linked together primarily by their adherence to the rule of life and the doctrines of their master. Pythagoras himself died around the turn of the century; the Pythagorean brotherhoods in Croton and other cities of Great Greece continued to flourish, and often dominated political life, until they provoked violent reaction and their own eventual destruction.

The contemporary testimony about Pythagoras consists of two or three fragments of Heraclitus, and one of Xenophanes. Heraclitus is forthright:

> Much learning does not teach understanding; if it did, it would have taught Hesiod and Pythagoras, and again Xenophanes and Hecataeus (fr. 40);
> [Pythagoras was] the pioneer of swindles (fr. 81);
> Pythagoras, son of Mnesarchus, of all men practised inquiry the most, and making a selection [sc. from the results of his inquiries] he composed as his own a system of 'wisdom', a collection of much knowledge, a low deception (fr. 129).

The last of these may be spurious; in any case, Heraclitus saw in Pythagoras only a polymath who had not merely missed the truth but gone in for deliberate deception. Xenophanes was equally hostile, to judge by the satirical tone in which he relates his story (DK 21 B 7). Herodotus, writing in the second half of the fifth century, also follows at one place (IV 95) a source which saw Pythagoras as a trickster who imposed upon the credulous. Heraclitus, Xenophanes, and their contemporary the geographer and historian Hecataeus were all in the Milesian tradition of free and rational inquiry and discussion. Pythagoras, it is clear, was something quite different. This is confirmed by the little that is reliably known of his sect. Some testimony, it is true, presents the early Pythagorean school as a centre of astronomical and mathematical research, in the same way as Plato's Academy was intended to be, but the more reliable tradition suggests that

Pythagoras and his followers were opposed in principle and in practice to free discussion and speculation, at least on fundamental questions. The words of the master had absolute authority.

It is reasonable, then, to ask why Pythagoras should occupy any space in a history of early Greek philosophy. No very con-confident answer can be given to this question; but it is possible, though by no means proved, that some of the ideas Pythagoras expounded may have influenced intellectual life in the Greek West at a time when it was about to produce some remarkable thinkers.

The best attested part of Pythagoras' teaching is that which concerned the souls of men and their destiny. The soul is a unity which is immortal; it is rational and responsible for its actions. Its fate is determined by those actions, as it lives through successive incarnations in human bodies or those of other animals or plants. By keeping itself pure, that is, free from the pollution of the bodily passions which beset it in these incarnations, it can eventually rise to its true or proper god-like state. But if it sins, it is punished and purified by prolonged suffering in more miserable incarnations. In other words, the soul is not at home in the body and must be kept apart from it as far as possible. These ideas are quite foreign to Greek tradition, and there has been much debate about their origins. In recent years, a good case has been made out for deriving them from the shamanism of tribes inhabiting the steppes of Asia. There are clear traces of shamanistic practices among the Thracians and the Scythians, from whom they would easily be transmitted to Greece.

From these beliefs it follows that the proper rule of life is asceticism. The Pythagorean societies in Great Greece were presumably communities who tried to follow this rule, but how strictly and logically this was done is not certain. For instance, it is not clear whether they abstained from all food which involved the taking of animal and vegetable life or not. The precepts which have survived under the name of *akousmata* appear to be genuinely Pythagorean, and these are largely taboo-prohibitions such as 'Do not stir the fire with a dagger', 'Do not look into a looking-glass with a lamp beside you', and the like. The procreation of children, and therefore marriage, was enjoined as a duty.

The Pythagoreans, though enemies of the body, did not withdraw from the everyday world. On the contrary, it is certain that they took part in the politics of their cities, and often a dominant part. The soul that abstains from the pleasures of the senses must be provided with other and worthier ways of using its time and energy, and political activity was one of these. It is clear that the energy and solidarity of the Pythagoreans made them a formidable political force, and it seems likely that they exercised their power with considerable austerity, which would account for the violent reactions against them in later years.

The other activities of the early Pythagoreans are covered in uncertainty. There is certainly a suggestion in the early sources that Pythagoras himself, if not his followers, claimed to exercise magical or miraculous powers, based on his acquisition of such supernatural knowledge and skills as are accessible to the initiated shaman. What is more doubtful is whether purely intellectual activity had any place in early Pythagorean life, and in particular the study of mathematics and astronomy. The earliest evidence on this point derives from the mid-fourth century, and is under suspicion of being a Platonising interpretation. Aristotle, it is true, knew of a group which he refers to as 'the people called Pythagoreans', who worked in Italy and held that numbers and their properties were the key to the structure of the universe. Unfortunately, this group, whatever its relation to the early Pythagorean school, is likely to belong to the second half of the fifth century.

The direct evidence being of doubtful value, it is necessary to look at the indirect indications given by what is known otherwise of the history of particular studies in Greece at this time.

In the history of mathematics there is a gap in our knowledge between the highest level reached by Babylonian arithmetic, algebra, and geometry before 1000 B.C. and the emergence of Greek arithmetic and geometry as intellectual disciplines in their own right. The gap is not one of time, since Babylonian mathematics remained essentially the same for hundreds of years, and was still in being under Persian rule in the fifth century, to the last half of which belong the first certain achievements of Greek mathematics. The first mathematician known to us as an individual is Hippocrates of Chios* who composed an 'Elements of Geometry' at some time in the last decades of the fifth century. With this work, if not before, geometry became a system of abstract thought. Of the development of arithmetic less is known, but it must have reached the same kind of stage about the same time. The gap between Babylonian and Greek mathematics is that between the accumulation of rules for the solution of concrete problems and the further step to a self-contained abstract system. This further step the Babylonians, to our knowledge, never took.

There are therefore two main problems: that of the transmission, if any, of Babylonian knowledge to Greece, and that of the origins of pure mathematics in Greece. There is no overwhelming necessity to include the early Pythagoreans under either head. All that can be said is that they were well posted, in time and space, to be influential in the development of mathematics in Greece, and that a number of small indications, each of little value separately, converge to suggest that they were so. It was precisely in the lifetime of Pythagoras that the importance of numbers and proportions for the structure of things was beginning to be realised. Signs of this appear in Heraclitus, who as has been seen was feeling his way towards the concept of 'structure', and who certainly thought proportions important. A polymath of this time, such as Pythagoras, would discover that numbers and proportions were of importance in several apparently unconnected branches of experience: in music, metallurgy, the visual arts and medicine. In music, the connection between musical intervals and arithmetical ratios was probably known, though the stories directly linking Pythagoras with the discovery must be considered legend. In metallurgy, the formulae for producing various alloys

---

*Not to be confused with his contemporary namesake, the great medical man Hippocrates of Cos.

were of course known to those who produced those alloys, and
Heraclitus seems to have paid attention to them. In sculpture, and
the visual arts generally, it is precisely in the late sixth and early
fifth century that the decisive steps are taken towards a realistic
rendering of the human body and other natural objects, an enterprise impossible without an awareness of the vital importance of
proportions between lengths. In medicine, the periodicity observable in certain diseases deeply impressed the earliest Greek medical men, and, in general, cycles in human and animal life began to
be noticed. Here again Heraclitus may be adduced, if in fixing the
length of a 'Great Year' he reasoned by analogy from the cycle of
human reproduction. All these sources of interest in numbers and
proportions reappear in those thinkers of the Greek West in the
early fifth century about whom anything is known, notably
Alcmaeon, Parmenides and Empedocles, who will be discussed
later in this chapter. Given these facts, it may be significant that
mathematical studies would fit well with the Pythagorean way of
life, and that Aristotle's 'Pythagoreans', who were certainly interested in (indeed, obsessed by) numbers, claimed to be followers
of Pythagoras, and this in Italy at a time not long after the break-
ing up of the original school. There is perhaps a relic of early
Pythagorean number-lore in the mysterious *tetraktus* or 'four-
some', esoterically associated with the Delphic oracle, musical
harmony, and the Sirens. All these considerations suggest that
numbers, at least, if not geometry, played some part in the teachings of Pythagoras and the activities of his school. But there is no
important advance in mathematics that can with any certainty at
all be attributed to them, not even 'Pythagoras' theorem'; it seems
likely that their number-lore was more number-mysticism than
arithmetic, but that they stimulated even so an interest in numbers
for their own sake and an awareness of their importance in the
structure of things.

With astronomy the case is similar. A great deal is known of
the Babylonian achievements. The Babylonians named many
individual fixed stars and constellations, distinguished the five

planets known in antiquity* as 'wanderers' relative to the fixed stars, and made some progress with the study of the motions of sun, moon and planets. They recognised the cardinal fact that all seven of these bodies have apparent paths confined to a small band of the heavens, occupied by the twelve constellations of the zodiac, which they distinguished and named. For computing the motions of the sun and moon, which particularly interested them, they contrived simple mathematical methods of fair accuracy.

Various indications suggest that some of this knowledge percolated to Greece *via* Ionia in the sixth century. Astronomy was not a principal interest of the Milesians or Heraclitus, whose concern was with the wider issues of cosmology, but Thales and Anaximander were perhaps involved in the transmission of knowledge. In the Greek West, before 450, there occurs the first Greek contribution to astronomy: a fragment of Parmenides (fr. 15, cf. fr. 14) shows that the reflection of the sun's light by the moon was known to him, and it is therefore probable that the cause of lunar eclipses was also. This in turn would be likely to suggest the true cause of solar eclipses and the key fact of the sphericity of the earth, but this can only be conjecture. The arguments for bringing in the early Pythagoreans to help to bridge the gap between Babylonia and fifth-century Great Greece are analogous to those in the case of mathematics, and so is the most reasonable conclusion: that the Pythagoreans attached special importance to the heavenly bodies, particularly the seven 'wanderers', and that this stimulated investigation by others outside the Pythagorean circle. Again, we have some scraps of relevant Pythagorean lore: the sun and moon were 'the isles of the blest', the planets were 'the hounds of Persephone', the Pleiades 'the lyre of the Muses', and the Great and Little Bears were 'the hands of Rhea'—descriptions which hint at esoteric doctrine which was intended to be meditated rather than discussed or criticised, but which might still serve to stimulate interest in the things described.

*

* Mercury, Venus, Mars, Jupiter, Saturn.

The theoretical study of music goes naturally with mathematics. It has already been said that the connection had probably been made by the time of Pythagoras, and may have contributed to his number-mysticism. There are also stray hints of a connection between music and the heavenly bodies being alleged by the early Pythagoreans.

In these fields, therefore, it is probable that the early Pythagoreans held certain doctrines derived from the strange mind of Pythagoras, but made no contribution to the advance of thought or knowledge except indirectly by provoking the investigations of others. Some light on the Pythagorean attitude to knowledge can perhaps be derived from the fragments of Empedocles of Acragas in Sicily, a unique figure whose poems cannot be dated much if at all later than 450.

Unlike any other Presocratic thinker of whom we have substantial knowledge (except perhaps Parmenides), he both belongs to the tradition of cosmological speculation subject to rational criticism and puts himself outside it. He was indisputably the author of two poems, both of which were read and admired until late in antiquity and of which there remain many fragments. In one poem—later given the title 'On Nature'—there is a cosmology which can be seen as an attempt to carry on the Milesian tradition in spite of the arguments which had been put forward by Parmenides against all cosmologies. This is how the cosmology of Empedocles will be treated in Chapter Seven, together with other enterprises of the same kind. In the other poem, later known as the 'Purifications', there is an account of the fate of the individual soul, its fall from a state of innocence by surrender to 'the temptations of Strife', its punishment by successive incarnations in which it feels itself a homeless exile, and the way to its eventual reinstatement in divine bliss. All this is manifestly close to Pythagorean teaching, as are many of the details, and there is no hint of any cosmology, laws of nature, or analysis of all things into indestructible elements; in the 'Purifications' the order of the universe is a purely moral one, the soul is a unitary, free and responsible agent, and no hint is given that it can be analysed into components other than itself. It is extremely difficult to construct any framework of ideas into which the statements of both poems can be simultaneously fitted, and in this sense there is a discrepancy between them, even if there is no formal contradiction.

In the face of this discrepancy, it is possible to suppose that Empedocles at some time experienced a 'conversion', which caused him to reject cosmology of the Milesian kind for Pythagorrean doctrines of the soul, or *vice versa*. Such a conversion is possible, but there is no independent evidence for it. Alternatively, there may be some way of showing that the discrepancy does not matter. If this possibility is to be explored, it is necessary to look more carefully at the two poems, and not merely at the propositions they advance but also the attitude that they imply towards those propositions.

It is not irrelevant to begin by pointing out the originality of Empedocles *as a poet*. He writes in hexameters, the metre of the Homeric epic and of Hesiod, and yet he creates a completely individual style which owes little to either. His style alone is enough to guarantee the unity of authorship of the two poems; it is rich, brilliant, declamatory and takes every kind of subject-matter in its stride with equal ease, from the torments of the fallen soul to the mechanism of respiration. It is a way of writing that has its dangers; if the poet is too self-indulgent it will quickly become unbearably hollow and noisy. So far as can be judged, Empedocles avoided such dangers by sticking closely to his subject-matter and not running on to too great length. This style conceals like a mask the attitude of Empedocles to his subject-matter. Only in one or two fragments of the 'Purifications' does some private emotion seem to be discernible. In the cosmological poem, it often seems as though Empedocles were writing simply in order to display his poetic gifts on a difficult subject.

Something further, however, can be learnt by looking at the forms into which the two poems are cast. The cosmological poem is addressed to Empedocles' young friend Pausanias, and has the form of instruction given to him about the nature of the world. This didactic form was not new in Greek literature, but it had not, so far as is known, been used for conveying cosmology before. Among the introductory and concluding remarks are some which are also novel in a Presocratic context. Pausanias is urged not to reveal what he is about to be told, and finally a series of truly remarkable promises is made to him:

> If you press them [these teachings] firmly in a shrewd mind, and contemplate them in a well-disposed mood, making this your undisturbed exercise, then all these teachings will surely remain with you so long as you live, and you will acquire besides from them much further knowledge; for these teachings grow of themselves to be part of the individual character, according to the natural disposition of each recipient. But if you go after other things, such as there are in thousands in human life, wretched things that blunt the concern for thought, then after some time these teachings will all at once desert you, in their desire to regain their own kindred. For you must know that everything has thought, and a share of intelligence (fr. 110).
>
> You shall learn all the medicines that keep off illness and old age; for you alone will I perform all this. You shall still the untiring winds, that rush over the earth and blow to ruin the tilled fields; and then again you shall if you wish change about and bring on winds again; you shall give men an opportune drought instead of dark rain, and streams of rain from heaven to nourish the trees instead of drought in summer; and you shall bring back from Hades the life of a dead man (fr. 111).

These words, and their didactic context, show clearly that the purposes of Empedocles in expounding his cosmology are widely different from those of any Ionian thinker. Pausanias is not expected to discuss critically in public what he is told, but to hold it fast and contemplate it as received truth, without even divulging it to others. It is true that there is room for further discoveries, but the foundations may not be challenged. This is Pythagorean practice, not Milesian. A further similarity with Pythagoreanism is given by the suggestion that the contemplation of the truths accepted is itself a kind of purification of the soul, an escape from the useless external cares of mankind. Even more strangely different from Ionian ways of thinking is the promise of practical results in fr. 111. This is not the first prophecy of the fruits of applied science, for the cosmological ideas of the poem could not possibly justify such presumptuous confidence. Pausanias is promised control of the weather, of illness, old age and death—in other words he will become a magician. In making the promise, Empedocles is claiming, most explicitly by saying 'for you alone will I perform all this', that he himself is a person of occult powers. Here the shamanistic sides of Pythagoreanism seem to be close at hand; what is startling is to find the purposes of initiation sub-served by a superficially rational cosmology, which is here treated as a magical object, the contemplation of which helps the soul to detach itself from external concerns.

From this point of view the discrepancy between the cosmo-logical poem and the 'Purifications' becomes less important, and further elucidation is provided by some other remarks. 'You shall learn,' Empedocles promises Pausanias, 'to the extent that mortal thought has bestirred itself' (fr. 2); that is, the cosmology is the product of the latest research, but a contrast is implied with some kind of higher knowledge, hinted at in the preceding lines, which is not accessible to mortal thought at all. Elsewhere, he invokes the Muse to tell him 'what it is fitting for short-lived men to learn' (fr. 3). It seems possible, then, that the 'Purifications' represents a higher kind of truth, not accessible to rational thought, and which supersedes, rather than contradicts, the cosmology.

The fragments of the 'Purifications' themselves give some sup-port to this view. In order to proclaim truths not accessible to men, Empedocles would have to be a divine being, which is precisely what he claims in the opening lines of the poem:

Friends, who inhabit the upper town in the great city on the honey-coloured hill of Acragas, and practise a good rule of life, respectfully sheltering guests and abstaining from wickedness, hail to you! I go about among you all, an immortal god, no longer a mortal man, receiving due honours, crowned with triumphal headbands and heaped with green garlands . . . (fr. 112, part).

We expect divine revelations after this beginning. They are to be made to a group of 'friends', who clearly are not the whole citizen body of Acragas, but, from the description, a small community of a Pythagorean kind in the city. Empedocles' claims are backed by his gifts of healing and prophecy, for which he is famous:

... When I come to splendid cities, the men and women revere me, and follow me in thousands to ask me the way to their own benefit, some desiring prophecies, while others inquire to hear helpful words for all kinds of diseases, being long pierced by severe pains (fr. 112, part).

The revelations that follow are largely in agreement with what is known of Pythagorean teaching, though the restrictions on animal food may be stricter and more logical than those of Pythagoras himself. Pythagoras is eulogised, without being named, as a man of surpassing wisdom, but there is no suggestion that he is the sole authority.

The attitude of Empedocles towards the study of nature suggests that Pythagoras and his original disciples also may very well have used cosmology for magical purposes. It is interesting that the same combination of shamanistic magic, esoteric doctrines about the after-life, political activity and the study of nature is to be found in the Taoists of ancient China, who provide many suggestive parallels to what is known of the Pythagoreans.

Empedocles is one of three thinkers of the Greek West who are at least partly independent of Pythagoras and who all seem to belong to the first half of the fifth century. The other two are Parmenides of Elea, a philosopher of extreme originality and power, whose greatest achievements will be considered in the next chapter, and Alcmaeon of Croton, a lesser but interesting figure, who will now be considered in connection with the development of medical and biological thought in the West at this time.

From Herodotus (III 131) we learn that, around 500, the medical men of Croton, the adopted city of Pythagoras, were the best in the Greek world. 'Of things in human life, what displays most wisdom? Medicine' was a piece of Pythagorean lore. The connections between asceticism, physical training and bodily health have always been obvious. In the half-century that followed, whether under Pythagorean influence or not can hardly be decided, speculative theories about the more striking phenomena of human and animal physiology began to be advanced. From the reports we have about Parmenides, Empedocles and Alcmaeon, some of these developments can be reconstructed; they are also illuminated by some of the late fifth-century medical writings which were largely influenced by them.

The single most important idea of this period in biology and medicine was that of a 'due mixture' (*krasis*) of component forces as the necessary and sufficient condition for the proper functioning of any organism. This concept clearly has some kinship with the *harmoniē* of Heraclitus; it explains orderly functioning by the existence of an internal structure which is complex but, in principle, mathematically determinable, and which somehow incorporates and reconciles naturally opposed forces. The concept of *krasis* was immensely influential in the theory of disease of later Greek and early modern writers. In Alcmaeon it is already found as the basis of an analogy between medicine and politics, between the animal body and the body politic. (This analogy too is perhaps implicit in Heraclitus fr. 114.) In the animal body, according to Alcmaeon, the 'powers' which are compounded are the familiar 'opposites': hot-cold, wet-dry, and perhaps others, for instance sweet-bitter. These are conceived of as agents of change acting upon their environment; they are all necessary in the body, but somehow are subject to a system of checks and balances so that their action is confined within their proper limits. This system is the *krasis*. In the city, the 'powers' are the various factions and interests, most obviously rich and poor. If, in either case, the delicate balance is disturbed, the action of some 'powers' will be excessive, and will impede the vital functions necessary for survival; in the animal body, these are especially digestion and respiration.

Though the precise mechanism of *krasis* was necessarily left vague, the concept rightly had great influence. It appears in Parmenides and Empedocles as well as in Alcmaeon, the interest of Empedocles in the due proportions of mixtures in various organic systems being particularly clear.

In these three thinkers there is also found a new interest in some of the obviously important functions of the living organism: nutrition, respiration, reproduction, and perception. The volume of information is greatest for the problems concerned with reproduction. The most obvious problem about animal reproduction is how it manages to produce new individuals which are recognisably of the same species as their parents and furthermore inherit particular personal characteristics of their parents or remoter ancestors. It is natural to postulate something that carries what would now be called 'genetic information', and that is contributed by both parents; this is called '*sperma*' by the thinkers in question. Then one must ask such questions as: how is the *sperma* formed in the body? what determines the sex of the child, and in general what it inherits from each parent? Theories of some detail about these further questions were already being discussed in Great Greece before 450. For digestion, the basic model seems to have been that of cooking, in which the action of heat in particular separated useful from useless ingredients of good, and produced a *krasis* among the useful ones. Of the mechanism of respiration there is an elaborate account in Empedocles (fr. 100) using the analogy of the behaviour of water in a simple device used for transferring small amounts of water from vessel to vessel. And on sense-perception there are again reports (esp. DK 28 A 46, 31 A 86) of theories advanced by Parmenides and Empedocles, of small sophistication even by Aristotle's standards, but interesting as the first attempts on a difficult problem. This is not the place for further details of the various hypotheses, nor for other more general ideas such as that apparently due to Alcmaeon, of the importance of the brain for the general regulation of bodily functions. Alcmaeon also appears as the father of an idea, which may perhaps be older, that there is an

intrinsic connection between eternity and motion in a circle. The
fixed stars, and the species of animals, both go through unending
circles, and individual men die 'because they cannot join the
beginning to the end'. It is possible that Pythagoras taught some
doctrine of eternal cyclic recurrence.

There was, then, in Great Greece at this time a continuing and
fruitful debate on basic questions of biology and medicine. Man,
and the animal kingdom, are for the first time fully a subject for
science, or at least the *bodily* aspects of men and animals are. It is
natural to connect this with the Pythagorean concept of the soul,
as something totally alien to the body, and having no necessary
connection with it. If what was of value in man was not human
at all, but an exiled divinity, this would facilitate and justify the
detached inspection of the facts of human physiology, as just
another part of cosmology.

Indeed, if any formula could ever sum up the intellectual
development of a period of years, then the years from around 530
to around 450, in Greece, might be brought under the formula
'the detachment of the soul from the body'. At least it seems to
be suggestive of interesting connections between many important
developments of the time. It can be applied literally to the teachings of Pythagoras and of others, including those grouped under
the vague heading of 'Orphics'. But in Heraclitus too this detachment of the divine soul from the 'natural' body has already
proceeded some distance. More widely, there is the emergence,
both in Heraclitus and in the West, of a concept of 'reason' or
'reasoned argument' as the proper way to truth, with a corresponding depreciation or even denial of the evidence of the senses;
here again, the reasoning part of man is in effect partly detached
from the bodily sensations which surround it. Correspondingly,
the object of the best kind of knowledge is refined from a physical
presence or force to a *structure*, and the branch of the study of
'structure in itself' which is pure mathematics shows signs of
appearing. It is only superficially in contradiction with this that,
at the same time, the human body becomes as never before an
object of study. In a parallel way, in the visual arts, the human

body and other things are rendered with a naturalness never before achieved, and this is done by a consciousness of the importance of structure in the form of proportions. Naturally, this 'formula' is to be taken as a means for grouping suggestively some of the thoughts that were 'in the air', not as a magic key to everything that was happening at this period. But the most profound expression of thought in these years has still to be considered: the philosophy of Parmenides of Elea, which is the subject of the next chapter.

CHAPTER FIVE

Parmenides and Zeno

THE foundation, around the year 540, of the city of Elea in south-ern Italy has already been mentioned. The city settled down to an undistinguished and provincial history. But in philosophy, at least, its name is as immortal as any other, on account of two of its citizens who were active as thinkers in the first half of the fifth century: Parmenides and his pupil Zeno, the former born in all probability about 515, the latter about 490.

Parmenides is the first Presocratic of whose thought we still have a nearly complete and continous exposition in his own words. That this is so is due entirely to one man, the Neoplatonist scholar Simplicius. In his commentary on the *Physics* of Aristotle, written early in the sixth century A.D., Simplicius quotes large extracts from the poem of Parmenides, in illustration of Aristotle's remarks on it, expressly because, as he says, the book had become scarce. It is therefore almost possible to approach Parmenides in the way intended by Parmenides himself; this chapter will follow that way as far as it can be established.

It is worth noticing that Parmenides expressed his thought in hexameter verses. This was not an odd or ridiculous thing to do, as it would be if a modern philosopher wrote in verse. Verse was still appropriate, and felt to be appropriate, for any pronounce-ment intended to be particularly memorable. Written books existed, and many states displayed their laws and decrees publicly in writing; yet the habit of relying on the written word was not widespread or of long standing. An educated man was one who had things by heart, and verse is more easily memorised than prose.

Yet the Milesians composed prose treatises, perhaps because of the intractability for verse of some of their subject-matter, perhaps in reaction against the poets generally as the authors of falsehoods. They were followed by such different figures as Pherecydes of Syros, who narrates his mythology in deliberately plain style, and Heraclitus, who aims at being memorable and employs in prose many of the artifices of poetic diction. It is difficult to see why, unless they had special intentions, Pherecydes and Heraclitus should not have employed verse, as Xenophanes did, and conversely it is perhaps a little surprising that Parmenides does write in verse. His hexameters are vigorous but not graceful, and often downright clumsy; he had no particular talent for verse. Above all, his arguments, being so novel, needed the clearest expression he could give them. In order to express them at all, he needs to strain the resources of the Greek language of his time; and that he chose to add to this difficulty that of fitting his words into hexameters is not easily explained. This problem may be connected with that of the intentions behind the introductory part of the poem, and the device which Parmenides employs of putting his thoughts into the mouth of a divine personage—the goddess Justice (*Dikē*).

What remains of the introduction runs as follows:

The horses that carry me along used to bring me as far as ever my desire reached, whenever the goddesses led and took me on to the road of many wise words, the road that carries the man who knows through all cities—along that road was I borne, for that way the understanding horses used to take me, pulling at the chariot, and the girls would lead the way. The axle in its naves gave out the squeak of the axle-pipe, and glowed with heat as it was pressed hard on either side by the two rounded wheels, each time that there came hurrying to escort me into the light the daughters of the sun, leaving the halls of Night, and thrusting aside with their hands the veils from their heads.

There is the gate of the paths of Night and Day, and this gate is surrounded by a lintel and a stone threshold; the airy gate itself is filled by large double doors, of which much-punishing Justice holds the alternate keys. Justice it was whom the girls addressed with soft words, and cunningly persuaded to thrust instantly aside from the gate for them the bolt with its iron peg; whereupon the gate opened, making a yawning gap between the leaves of the door, and making the richly-bronzed doorposts, fitted with nails and pivots, twist in alternate directions in their sockets. This way, then, straight through the gates, the girls drove the horses and chariot along the path.

Then the goddess welcomed me kindly, took in her hand my right hand, and addressed me, speaking thus: 'Young man, who in company with immortal chariot-drivers come to our house with the horses that carry you, hail! for no bad destiny is it that sent you out to come this way—it is indeed a way remote from the paths of men—but that which is right and just. You are to learn everything: both the immoveable heart of well-rounded truth, and the opinions of mortal men, in which there is no truly convincing force—still, that too you shall learn, how these opinions are to cover everything in acceptable fashion.' (fr. 1)

The pattern exemplified here—a journey by a human being to a divine one, who tells him what he wishes to know—is widespread in folktale and was already familiar in Greek literature. There is therefore a certain atmosphere of literary artifice in this introduction; but the clumsy, jolting, vigorous movement of the verses manages to convey an impression of Parmenides' total absorption in the experience which he is describing. To explain what that experience was, it is natural to attempt an allegorical interpretation. Allegory as a self-conscious device was already recognised, for allegorical interpretation of Homer was being practised by Theagenes of Rhegium. It is natural to begin by taking the journey to represent the progress along a line of investigation, since in the later part of the poem words meaning 'road' or 'path' are repeatedly used to mean 'line of reasoning'. From this it is possible to build up a quite plausible system of interpretation: the horses are Parmenides' reasoning power; the girls, the daughters of the Sun, are the element of illumination or intuition without which reasoning power cannot make the crucial steps; the passage through the gate, which divides the paths of Night and Day, is then the passage from one line of reasoning to another, one false and one true —these can be identified a little later in the poem. And the goddess

Justice, who keeps the gate and expounds the truth, is, as in Heraclitus, the guaranteeing power who sees to it that things are as they must be.

Even if this interpretation is essentially correct, there is still the question why Parmenides chose to introduce his thought by placing it in this setting. Like the use of verse rather than prose, this seems to be a way of putting it at one or two removes from the ordinary world. As will be seen, Parmenides did indeed have good reason for doing just this, since in his opinion the ordinary world was totally unreal. An introduction of the kind usual in a prose work: 'These are the sayings of Parmenides of Elea,' for example, might have exposed him to the charge of self-contradiction, and would not have conveyed his sense of possessing a new method, independent of all that constituted ordinary experience, and critical of it.

The central section of the poem follows, in which the goddess expounds to Parmenides 'the steadfast heart of well-rounded truth'. Thanks to Simplicius, almost all of this part is preserved, and it is beyond doubt that its plan is as follows. Two 'paths of inquiry' are propounded as being the only conceivable ones; one is stated to be 'the path of (true) persuasion', and one is called 'quite undiscoverable' and an argument to this conclusion is given, after which the second path is considered to have been eliminated. Then a third path is mentioned, as being that taken by ordinary men, but this is at once dismissed as plainly self-contradictory. Finally, the one remaining path is accepted and its consequences are explored.

The introduction of the first two paths is as follows (the goddess is speaking to Parmenides, as in all the further fragments):

Come then, I will tell (and do you take in the story you hear) the ways of inquiry which alone are to be thought of: the first, that says that (it) is and that it cannot be that (it) is not—this is the path of true persuasion, for it follows the truth; the second, that says that (it) is not and that it must be that (it) is not—*this* track, I tell you, is quite undiscoverable . . . (fr. 2, part).

Since the paths are lines of inquiry, it is not surprising to find them identified by their starting-points, that is, the premisses from which the inquiry begins in each case. The great difficulty is to determine the meaning of these two premisses. One has been rendered: 'that (it) is and that it cannot be that (it) is not'; the other: 'that (it) is not and that it must be that (it) is not'. The bracketing of 'it' is designed to make the translation as non-committal as possible between two alternative kinds of interpretation. The indicative verb *esti*, and its negation, can in Greek stand alone, as a complete sentence, without any *expressed* subject (unlike 'is' in English). But in order that this sentence should be intelligible, it is necessary that the context should supply an implied subject; otherwise, *esti* and its negative make no more sense than 'is' and 'is not' by themselves in English.

There are therefore two possible kinds of interpretations here: one is to suppose that a subject or subjects to *esti* and its negative here can somehow be supplied from the context, and was intended by Parmenides to be so supplied; the other, that Parmenides was deliberately departing from ordinary usage, and straining the resources of the language, by introducing these words, for some particular purpose of his own, without subjects. Both kinds of interpretation have had adherents. The question is so fundamental to the understanding of Parmenides that it must be treated at length.

At this point, of all points, in his poem, it would seem wildly improbable that Parmenides should fail to be as explicit as possible. If, then, a subject is intended to be supplied, it should be easily retrievable from the context. It is possible to suppose that lines immediately preceding fr. 2, which have not been preserved, announced the subject of these paths. If fr. 2 itself is considered, the only subject which can easily be supplied in each case is 'the path'. This would mean that each path began with a premiss *about itself*: one said 'I am, and it cannot be that I am not': the other said 'I am not, and it must be that I am not'.

If a subject is not intended to be supplied, two reasons suggest themselves for this: one, that *esti* and its negation, and the two paths of inquiry, are intended to apply to *any* subject whatever that may be proposed; the other, that Parmenides holds that *no* subject whatever *can* be talked about until the choice between paths has been made.

It is obvious that the choice from among the possibilities set out in the last two paragraphs, and others less plausible, can be made only in the light of the whole of this part of the poem. In order to see what the premisses mean, it is necessary to see what deductions are made from them, and what more is said about each of the paths.

A further difficulty about the meaning of *esti*, and its negation, is that the verb *einai* of which it is a part has all the main uses of the English 'to be' and some further ones. If used absolutely, with a subject and nothing else, it normally means 'exists'; but can (applied to something spoken or thought) mean 'is true'. Used not absolutely, it may, like 'is', be a copula or be used in a predication. It is difficult to see good reason for bringing any but the 'existential' use into play in the discussion of Parmenides, yet other uses have been thought to be relevant and the possible interpretations are thereby multiplied.

Of the elimination of the path '(it) is not' a certain amount remains:

... the second, that says that (it) is not and that it cannot be that (it) is not—*this* track, I tell you, is quite undiscoverable. For you could neither know what is not (that is not feasible) nor speak of it. For the same thing is there to be thought and is there to be. ... What is there to be spoken of and thought, must be, for it is there to be, while that which is not is not there. These things I bid you mark well. From this path, then, of inquiry first I block you ... (frr. 2, part, 3, 6, part).

This translation begs certain questions (which cannot here be discussed) about the meaning and arrangement of the words that have been preserved. It yields the following argument:

A. The conclusion of the argument is that the path is 'quite undiscoverable' (*panapeuthea*). This, apparently, is in itself a sufficient reason for rejecting it. To see what this means, it is sufficient to consider that a path that cannot be discovered at all, even though we seem to know its starting-point, is one that cannot *exist*. There can be no path with such a starting-point. A later summary of the same argument says: 'The decision . . . is already made: namely, to leave alone the one path, as being unthought [or: unthinkable] (*anoēton*) and nameless—for it is not a genuine path—and to take the other as being real and true.' (fr. 8, part).

B. The proximate reason for this conclusion is then given by the words: 'For neither could you know what is not (that is not feasible) nor speak of it'. In order to move from here to the conclusion, it is necessary also to know that, if the path existed, it would involve knowing or speaking of what is not, whether truly or falsely. But this is immediately obvious, since the starting-point of the alleged path, '(it) is not', involves speaking or thinking about *something* which is not, on any of the interpretations previously offered. So the last step in the argument is clear and persuasive.

C. It remains for Parmenides to give a proof of the thesis that what is not cannot be known or spoken of (or thought of); or, as he rephrases it, that what can be thought and spoken of, must be. The proof, such as it is in the fragments, is contained in the words: 'The same thing is there to be thought and is there to be' (*to gar auto noein estin te kai einai*), and: 'What is there to be spoken of and thought of, must be, for it is there to be, while that which is not, is not there to be.'

At this point, Parmenides uses a Greek idiom which, perhaps fortunately, is very similar to the English idiom in such phrases as 'there is water to drink' in the sense of 'water which can be drunk is at hand', or (less idiomatic in English) 'there are soldiers to fight' in the sense of 'soldiers who can do some fighting are at hand'. Parmenides uses this idiom, and gives it a peculiar twist in the phrase 'it is there to be', which plays a crucial part in the reasoning. His claim, which he appears to regard as self-evidently correct, is that whatever 'is there to be thought of', necessarily 'is there to be', and that this, in turn, means not merely that it *can* be, but that it *is*. No further justification is given for these two steps in what remains.

It seems plausible to suppose that Parmenides did indeed take the step from 'it is there to be thought of' *via* 'it is there to be' to 'it is' as self-evidently valid. For it is a way of reasoning which in various forms has had a powerful appeal for philosophers of many periods. How *do* we succeed, it may be asked, in talking (as apparently we do) about unreal or impossible things like unicorns or round squares? The fact that apparently meaningful sentences can be uttered about them seems to show that we do succeed in talking and thinking about them; but then some reference has been made to them, and then there must exist, in some sense, the thing to which reference has been made. One cannot refer to what is not there to be referred to, any more than one can point at something that is not there to be pointed at. This is a fundamental difficulty that any philosophical account of language must be equipped to account for. The idiom used by Parmenides brings out the difficulty very well, but it would be wrong to suppose that it causes the difficulty to arise.

The reconstruction of the argument against the path '(it) is not' may be summarised thus: to take the path '(it) is not' involves speaking of or thinking of something that is not; but what can be spoken or thought of, is; hence, it is not possible to take the path '(it) is not', even in the sense of placing oneself at its starting-point, so that the path cannot exist at all. In other words, the premiss '(it) is not' is not shown to be false; it is shown to be not a possible premiss at all, since it not an expression of any possible thought. It is meaningless. The same is true, *a fortiori*, of the second part of the premiss, 'it must be that (it) is not'.

The argument to show that '(it) is not' is meaningless throws some light on a problem which has so far been disregarded: the problem of why Parmenides supposes the two paths to be the only conceivable paths of inquiry. Suppose some other starting-point to be propounded; then, Parmenides would argue, this premiss must say something about something (say X), so it commits you to saying that X is. Therefore, to say of X that it is, is the least you can say about X, whatever X is. So the most fundamental inquiry possible is to see what one is committed to in saying or denying of anything that it is. This suggests '(it) is' and '(it) is not' as starting-points, but does not explain why they are expanded by the addition of '(it) cannot not-be' and 'it must be that (it) is not' respectively. To explain these additions, consider that they have the effect of excluding two further premisses: '(it) is, but need not be', and '(it) is not, but possibly can be'. It has been seen that the phrase 'it is there to be' is so used as to make it possible to prove that whatever can be, is. Given this principle, it is clear that '(it) is not, but possibly can be' is self-contradictory. Further, '(it) is, but need not be' would then be equivalent to '(it) is, but it may be that (it) is not and (therefore) *necessarily* is not', which is self-contradictory on any plausible view of modal logic.

Having eliminated the path '(it) is not', the goddess immediately introduces a third path not (as far as can be seen) previously mentioned, and dismisses it in turn:

... From this path [sc. '(it) is not')], then, of inquiry first I block you, but next from the following one, which has been forged by ignorant mortals, the two-headed creatures. Helplessness it is that steers the wandering minds in their breasts, and they drift along, deaf and blind, in confused throngs, like men amazed. They think that to be and not to be is the same thing and not the same thing—the path of all of them is back-turning (*palintropos*) ... For it shall never be brought about by any force, that things that are not should be. Fence off your thought from this path of inquiry, and do not let habit that comes from much experience force you along this path, making you wield an unlooking eye and an ear full of noise and a tongue likewise—but judge by *reason* (*logōi*) the controversial proof that I announce (fr. 6, part, fr. 7).

The new path, then, leads to self-contradiction in the forms 'to be and not to be are the same and not the same' and 'things that are not, are'. This suggests that the premiss was either '(it) is and (it) is not', which leads immediately to the second form of self-contradiction, and suggests the first; or '(it) is, but need not be' as above. Because the path is evidently self-contradictory, it is not a serious contender, which explains why it is omitted from the original statement of the paths. It is introduced here, as if by an afterthought, apparently because it is the path of ordinary men, and it is necessary to expose their mistakes. Parmenides does not say that men choose this path deliberately; rather, he insists, they wander along it with no proper awareness of what they are doing, deluded by habit and sense-perception. The invective is very like that of Heraclitus, for Parmenides like Heraclitus takes it that he has seen deeper into the structure of things than other men, by the aid of something which goes beyond sense-perception and reveals its insufficiency: by reasoning.

Sense-perception appears to tell men that there is a changing and diverse world around them and in them. As will become clear in fr. 8, Parmenides believes that change and multiplicity are impossible, because they involve an illegitimate assertion of '(it) is not' and of '(it) is' simultaneously. Hence ordinary men, who take the world to be much as it appears, are in fact, though they do not know it, committed to the path '(it) is and (it) is not' and for this reason fall into hopeless self-contradiction. This is the case of all men alike who allow any kind of change and multiplicity as real; therefore Heraclitus must be included in this condemnation, and there is some reason to suspect that Parmenides here has Heraclitus particularly in mind. There is every likelihood that Parmenides knew of the thought of Heraclitus; and if he did, it would be natural that he should see Heraclitus as the worst offender of all, a man who was not confusedly unaware of the self-contradictions, but was aware of them and gloried in them. At the climax of Parmenides' invective occur the striking words: 'of all of them the path is back-turning (*palintropos*)'—appropriate words to describe the path '(it) is and (it) is not', but also suggestive of Heraclitus, whose *palintropos harmoniē*, it has been argued, was an attempt to express a view of the ultimate structure of things in which a unity reconciles contraries, and whose way was 'up and down, one and the same'. It even seems quite possible that the whole of Parmenides' thought is a reaction against Heraclitean paradox, an attempt to see what can be said that will not involve the speaker in self-contradiction.

The elimination of the path '(it) is not', and the reduction of ordinary men's beliefs to an evident self-contradiction, leave the stage clear for the exploration of the one remaining path, '(it) is and it cannot be that (it) is not'. Fortunately, this exploration is preserved entire. In the following translation, the letters *A* to *E* have been inserted to label successive sections of the argument.

Only one story of a path is now left; namely, that (it) is. On this path there are very many signs, showing that what is is uncreated and indestructible, whole, unique, unmoved and perfect; nor was it, nor will it ever be, since it *is* all together now, one and coherent.

A. For what birth will you seek for it? By what way and from what did it grow up? And I will not allow you to say or think that it came from what is not; for it cannot be said or thought that it is not. Besides, what necessity, if it began from nothing, would have driven it on to come into being, sooner or later? (Thus, either it must be utterly or not at all.) Nor will the force of convincing proof ever allow that from what is there should come into being anything besides itself. Wherefore, Justice does not slacken the fetters to let it come to be, nor to let it be destroyed, but holds it fast. The decision on these matters lies in the following: (it) is or (it) is not—but the decision is already taken as is necessary; namely, to leave aside the one path as unthinkable and nameless, and to allow the other path to be and be true. How then could what is be subsequently destroyed? How could it come into being? For if it came into being, it is not; and likewise if it is about to be in the future. So coming-into-being has been quenched, and destruction is undiscoverable.

B. Nor is it divided, since it is all alike, and it is not any more or any less in any way, so as to prevent itself from being coherent, but it is all full of that which is. Therefore it is all coherent, for what is sticks close to what is.

C. Unmoved, then, in the limits of great bonds, it *is* without beginning, without ceasing, since coming-into-being and destruction are driven very far away, the true proof having thrust them aside. The same, remaining in the same, all by itself it lies, and so it remains firmly there; for strong Necessity holds it in the bonds of the limit (*peiratos*) that fences it about, because it is not right that what is should be without end, since it is not lacking in anything; if it were lacking, it would lack *everything*.

D. The same thing is to be thought of and is the thought that it is, for you will not find thinking apart from that which is, in which the thought is expressed. For there was, is, and shall be nothing else besides what is, since *that* has been bound by Fate to be whole and unmoved. Therefore everything will be mere name, all that mortal men, believing to be true, have established by convention as coming into being, being destroyed, being and not being, changing its place and altering its bright colour.

E. But since the limit (*peiras*) is at the extremes, it is complete from all sides, like the mass of a well-rounded ball, and evenly balanced every way from the centre. For it must not be any greater or any less in this way or that; since neither is there what is not, which would stop it from being joined together, nor is it possible that what is could be in one way more, in another way less, than what is, for all of it is free from imperfection, and, equal to itself from all directions, it meets its limits in a uniform way (fr. 8, 1–49).

The plan of this part of the poem is clear in outline. The first few lines contain a programme of what follows, giving a summary of what will be proved as a consequence of the premiss. Then, in sections *A* to *E*, a series of proofs is given, and it is clear that there is at least a rough correspondence between the programme and what is actually proved.

These proofs are the core of Parmenides' thought. Any attempt to understand them must begin with two basic questions.

First: does Parmenides believe he has shown that the path '(it) is' is a true path, or only that it is the only possibly true path? He certainly takes himself to have shown the latter. Suppose that '(it) is' is not true. Then either it is false, in which case '(it) is not' is true; but '(it) is not' is meaningless, so that it cannot be true. Hence, if '(it) is' is not true, it must be because it too is unthinkable. In this case, since all other thoughts involve the thought 'X is', for some X, it follows that no thought is possible at all. It is not clear whether or not Parmenides envisaged this possibility, but it is worth noticing that Aristotle took the possibility of thought to be a basic assumption of Parmenides. For Aristotle (*de Caelo* 298ᵇ 22f.) summarises the consequences of '(it) is' by saying that Parmenides and his followers thought it necessary to have a changeless object of thought 'if there is to be any knowledge or thought at all'. Parmenides himself speaks in at least two places as if the path '(it) is' and its consequences were known to be true absolutely: at the end of fr. 1 they are called 'the steadfast heart of well-rounded truth', and, in fr. 8, immediately after section *E*, the whole set of proofs from *A* to *E* is called a 'trustworthy reasoning and thought concerning truth'. In section *A* itself, the same point is made less clearly when Parmenides says: 'The decision is already taken, as is necessary: namely, to leave aside the one path as unthinkable and nameless, and to allow the other path to be and to be true.' This seems to say that the truth of '(it) is' is as necessary as the unthinkableness of '(it) is not'.

If it is correct that Parmenides takes '(it) is' to be true absolutely, one corollary is that he believes that true thought is possible, since what is true is thinkable. This has some relevance to the interpretation of section *D*.

The second basic question on the path '(it) is' is: of what grammatical subject are the various predicates proved to be true, and how do these subject-predicate propositions emerge from the original '(it) is'? To ask this is to recur to the problem of the subjects (if any) of '(it) is' and '(it) is not' in the first place. Since the argument against '(it) is not' makes it clear that adopting that path commits one to speaking and thinking about something that is not, by symmetry it follows that adopting '(it) is' commits one to speaking and thinking about something that is. In the exploration of '(it) is' nothing further is assumed about this subject of thought than the facts that it is, and that it can be thought about. When a phrase is needed to occupy the place of a grammatical subject, the words used are '*eon*' or '*to eon*', the neuter participle of *einai* with or without the definite article. This may be taken to mean 'that which is', *either* in the sense of 'whatever is' *or* in that of 'the thing that is'. The uncertainty here corresponds to the existence of the various possibilities about the original meanings of '(it) is' and '(it) is not'. If '(it) is' and '(it) is not' were originally intended to be said of a definite subject S, then '(it) is' means 'S is', and all that follows is demonstration of certain truths about S, using only the fact that S is, and can be thought of, and never once naming S by its true name. This is possible, but strangely implausible. In this case when '(*to*) *eon*' occurs, it means S, but must be translated 'the thing that is'. If '(it) is' and '(it) is not' are intended to be applied to *any* subject of discourse that may be supplied, then '(*to*) *eon*' means 'whatever is' and the fact that no individual thing is mentioned by name is explained by the fact that Parmenides is not talking about any particular thing, but about anything of which '(it) is' is asserted. And finally, if *no* subject of discourse is possible until the choice between '(it) is' and '(it) is not', then after the choice of '(it) is' it is plausible to say that the subject that arises from that choice is (*to*) *eon*, either in the sense of '*the* thing that is', or in that of 'whatever is'.

The upshot of this is that, whichever view is taken of the original meaning of '(it) is' and '(it) is not', the phrase '(*to*) *eon*' can be translated according to this view. Its use does not involve the assumption that there is only one thing that is. In fact it looks as if Parmenides thought he had supplied a proof of this somewhere in the exploration of '(it) is'—for the programme announces that it will be shown that that which is is *unique* (*mounogenes*). If this has to be proved, it cannot be known already; so the use of '(*to*) *eon*' cannot imply it. This interpretation of the path '(it) is' suggests strongly that it sets out by assuming that something or some things are, without prejudice as to what those are. This in turn tends to confirm those interpretations of the original choice according to which no particular subject is intended for '(it) is' and '(it) is not', so that they must come close to representing what might be expressed by 'for some x, x is' and 'for some x, x is not'.

*

The five sections labelled *A* to *E* must now be considered in turn.

In *A*, it is shown that whatever is is not subject to coming-into-being (*genesis*) or passing-out-of-being (*olethros*). For this necessarily involves there being something, other than whatever is, out of which what is comes to be, or into which it passes away. If this is other than whatever is, it must not-be, but then we are using something that is not as a factor in our explanation. This is impossible, since we *cannot* treat something that is not as a subject for thought; accordingly, *genesis* and *olethros* are inconceivable. For good measure, an argument is added to show that even if *genesis* were conceivable, it would offend against the Principle of Sufficient Reason: given that which is not, there would be no reason why *genesis* should occur rather than not, and why it should occur at some time rather than at another.

This much is clear, but the latter part of *A* is confusing, and contains difficulties of text and interpretation. Fortunately, this part seems to be entirely a recapitulation.

Section *B* is short, but of great importance. It shows that whatever is is 'coherent' (*xuneches*) and not divided (or divisible). This might be taken in either of two ways: (*a*) whatever is, is internally coherent; or (*b*) whatever is, is coherent with whatever else is, externally. If (*a*) is correct, then whatever is is shown to be a unity; if (*b*), then whatever is is proved unique, since all that is coheres. The ambiguity here is matched by the ambiguity in the reasons given: 'it is all alike', which might mean: 'whatever is, is all (internally) alike', or 'all that is, is alike'. To decide whether (*a*), or (*b*), or both, are intended, it is necessary to refer elsewhere. In the programme, as was seen, both 'whole' (*oulon*) and 'unique' (*mounogenes*) are promised. From the language in section *D*, it is clear that uniqueness has been previously proved. Accordingly the proof must either be here or in section *C*; but in section *C* it cannot plausibly be found. It seems necessary, therefore, to take section *B* as proving both 'internal' and 'external' coherence, and this conclusion is rather reinforced by the expression with which it concludes: 'whatever is sticks close to whatever is'.

The importance of section *B* is thus that it *proves* that there can be at most one subject of thought. For, given any subject of thought, which necessarily is, this cannot be separated either into parts or from whatever else is. From now on, then, it is immaterial whether we translate '(*to*) *eon*' as 'whatever is' or 'that which is'; the class of things that are contains just one member, namely, that which is.

The proof is achieved by considering the implications of separation. If something X that is is separate from something else Y that also is, then there must be a third thing Z, distinct from X and Y, to separate them. Z cannot be something that is not; but if Z is, then it is indistinguishable from X and Y and cannot separate them. That this is the structure of proof envisaged is shown by reference to section *E*, where the idea is stated more fully.

As stated, the proof does not seem entirely convincing. Why should not Z be, and yet be distinguishable from other things that are? Parmenides' reason is that what is does not allow variations of 'intensity', of more and less. Even granted this, it seems that there might be variations which were not of this kind. This point will be taken up later.

Section *C* also presents some difficulty. Following the argument backwards from the end of the section yields the following train of reasoning: (1) It (*to eon*) is not lacking in any respect; (2) Therefore it is not incomplete; (3) Therefore it has a limit (*peiras*); (4) Therefore it is unmoved and unvarying.

Step (1) is justified in the words: 'if it were lacking, it would lack everything'. It is not hard to see that the general principle referred to here is the same as that which underlies section *B*. Just as the only conceivable variations within what is are those of 'degree of being', so the only conceivable lack within what is is that of being, and since being does not admit of degrees, lack of being is complete failure to be, which is inconceivable.

Steps (2) and (3) go closely together. Since it is in no respect lacking, it is as complete as can be, and hence has a 'limit' (*peiras*).

The word *'peiras'* occurs in the earliest Greek literature with a variety of senses, but the common and basic notion underlying them all (see page 17) is that of something that marks or brings about the end or completion of something else. Thus it is used of the spatial limit of an area, the final decision of a dispute, the conclusion of an event, the means of achieving a result. It is not therefore surprising that in this section too *peiras* is 'the mark of completion': to have a *peiras* is to be complete, and conversely.

In step (4), the existence of the *peiras* is thought of as a constraint on that which is, just as if it were a physical boundary. What is necessarily complete, cannot vary, because that would be adding to it. If that which is is now different from what it will be, then it is not now complete, since there is more of it to come; it cannot at any time be about to vary, and therefore never varies. The thought here seems to be the same as what is expressed, in the 'programme', by the words: 'it *is*, all together, *now*'.

Section *D* appeals explicitly to the results of *B* and *C*. Since what is is whole and unchanging, nothing else is, was or shall be beside what is. Therefore thinking cannot be apart from what is—in other words, thinking must be an attribute of what is. Though the first line of this section is difficult to interpret, it seems to say this by stating that 'what can be thought of *is* the same thing as the thought'—in other words, that which is is a thought that thinks about itself. This statement, and the reasoning just given, depend upon the further premiss that thinking does occur— a premiss which, as has been seen, may reasonably be taken to be involved in the acceptance of the path '(it) is'.

From the fact that what is is a single unvarying whole, section *D* further deduces that the ideas of mortal men are radically mistaken. They believe that there are certain things which vary, and are diverse; not only is this false, but their beliefs are unthinkable —accordingly, what appear to be referring expressions in their talk make no reference whatever, and are 'mere name', that is, noises without significance.

*

Like section *D*, section *E* introduces no new ideas, but draws out the consequences of sections *B* and *C*. From the incoherent notions of ordinary men, the reader is brought back to a final presentation of that which is. Being complete and internally homogeneous, it is like a spherical ball, because 'it meets its boundaries uniformly'; the point of the comparison, as Parmenides makes clear, is the radial symmetry of the ball. Whether this is contemplated from the centre or from the outside, it presents the same aspect in every direction.

The general form of argument in the fundamental sections *A B* and *C* is clearly as follows: whatever is, is F (where 'F' is some predicate); for suppose not, then something is not-F; but to explain what it is for anything to be not-F involves the introduction of what is not into our account; hence, it is inconceivable that anything is not-F, so that whatever is, is F.

As has been pointed out, the applications made of this form of argument are not all totally convincing. It is not easy to see why the thought that what is is not homogeneous should involve the introduction of what is not: for we can conceive part of what is as being G (say), part of it as being not-G, where 'G' and 'not-G' are predicates involving no reference at all to what is not. And if this is conceivable, it is equally conceivable that what is should be all not-G, so that it would lack the property of being G, which it might conceivably have had.

It is clear in a general way that considerations such as these are alien to the spirit of Parmenides' thinking; but he does not seem to block them explicitly. In order to do so, he would need to claim generally that what is conceivable is the case. This is an idea which has certainly haunted much subsequent philosophy, in various forms, though not always openly avowed. It is closely allied with the idea that what is to qualify as truly real must have an 'official' characterisation, which it must live up to and not exceed —it must be exclusively *itself*. It is closely allied to theories which reduce predications to statements of identity, as Parmenides may implicitly have done. It certainly seems that he takes it that what

predications can be made depends entirely on what subjects there
are; in other words, that he admits the conceivability of 'whatever
is, is F' only if 'F' is *characteristic* of whatever is, i.e. if 'whatever
is, is not-F' is inconceivable. Hence 'whatever is, is F' is true if
and only if it can be proved true. The completeness principle
which results here is certainly hinted at elsewhere: the completeness of the system is claimed explicitly at the end of fr. 1—'you
are to learn *everything*'—and implicitly at the beginning, where
the horses are said to have brought Parmenides 'as far as ever my
desire reached'.

If the argument has been rightly understood, Parmenides shows
in these sections that that which is is a unity, unique, complete,
unchanging, homogeneous. Negatively, it is not many things,
which that which is is often supposed to be. It is clear that it is not,
in any ordinary sense, given to us by experience; experience,
derived from sense-perception, is precisely what Parmenides
warns against. That which is can be apprehended by reason alone.
  This being so, it is clear that that which is is not an occupier of
space or time in any usual sense. It is necessary, then, to explain
in metaphorical senses those expressions, used of that which is,
of which the normal application is to things in space or time.
Thus, in section *B*, the words 'it is all coherent; for what is sticks
close to what is' are at first sight applicable only to what occupies
space, but must be taken more abstractly and generally as stating
the unity in every respect of that which is. In section *C* the *peiras*
is talked about as if it were a spatial limit that constrained that
which is from moving; here a translation into abstract terms has
already been suggested. More troublesome is the talk of radial
symmetry in section *E*, because it seems to suggest that that which
is has a centre. It must be supposed that the point of saying these
things is that that which is is the same 'however you look at it'—
it presents always the same aspect, unlike the supposed components
of the ordinary world, which change according to the point of
view, as Heraclitus makes so clear. So too, such apparently time-
pregnant remarks as 'it remains firmly fixed' can be taken as

implying nothing more than the absence of any kind of variation
of that which is.

With the removal of the only possible subject of thought into
an abstract realm goes the denial of all reality to all occupants of
the ordinary world, as section *D* expressly states. The divorce
between appearance and reality has been made complete.

With the conclusion of all that can be said about the consequences of '(it) is', it might be thought that the poem of Parmenides would be at an end, since there is no more truth to be told.
But the preliminary remarks of the goddess in fr. 1 promised:
'You are to learn everything: both the immovable heart of well-
rounded truth, and the opinions of mortal men, in which there is
no truly convincing force—still, that too you shall learn, how
these opinions are to cover everything in acceptable fashion.' The
promise is now carried out; fr. 8 concludes:

At this point I end for you my trustworthy tale and thought concerning truth. From now on, learn the opinions of mortal men, by
listening to the deceitful ordering (*kosmon*) of my words.

Mortal men, then, have settled their decision to name two forms,
one of which they should not name—here they are mistaken—and
have separated them into opposite shapes, and laid down signs for
them distinct the one from the other. . . The whole of this plausible
world-ordering I declare to you, so that no knowledge of mortal men
shall ever overtake you (fr. 8, 50–6, 60–1).

What is to be expounded is evidently a system of cosmology, as
is further confirmed by the contents of the remaining fragments
of the poem, as well as the reports of later writers. It cannot
therefore represent the opinions of men in general, since they did
not adhere to a particular cosmological system. The passages that
have just been quoted suggest rather that Parmenides intends to
unite a number of generally accepted beliefs into a coherent
system, and to do this in such a way as to produce the best possible
cosmology. The criteria by which his efforts are to be judged are
implied to be (*a*) the coherence and degree of system, (*b*) the
inclusiveness and (*c*) the plausibility, that is, the correspondence

to observed phenomena, of the construction. Parmenides seems
to be the first to make explicit these nowadays familiar requirements for a scientific theory.

At the same time as Parmenides announces, in these passages,
his intention of competing with others in the problem of constructing a cosmology, he is careful to repeat that the results cannot be
true, but only 'plausible', or 'deceptive', or 'acceptable'. The
word which has been translated 'in an acceptable fashion' is
dokimōs, the adverb of the adjective *dokimos*, a two-faced word
originally applied to coined money, as it would seem, with the
sense 'acceptable tender', and neutral between the connotations
'genuine' and 'a good forgery'.

If cosmologies, all of which are for Parmenides strictly meaningless, can yet be more and less plausible, it must be because
they correspond well or badly with what appear to be the facts of
observation. The whole of ordinary experience, incompatible as
it is with the path '(it) is', cannot be anything but delusion; but
Parmenides seems here to admit that there is a structure and a
pattern in this delusion. The problem is how such an admission
can be made without inconsistency. To talk about appearances
and opinions is to treat them as objects of thought; but only that
which is can be an object of thought, and the diverse and changing world of appearances can hardly be identified with that which is.

Not only does there seem to be an inconsistency here, but if
there is it seems to be an unmotivated inconsistency. If Parmenides
has any confidence in the path '(it) is', he has no reason to trouble
himself with the contradictions of ordinary experience. No
adequate motivation appears anywhere in what is left of the poem.
Aristotle, discussing the cosmology, merely says (*Metaphysics*
986ᵇ 27–33) that Parmenides 'was compelled to go along with
the appearances' and that he 'supposed that, according to reason,
the one existed, but according to sense-perception, many things
existed'. The compulsion of which Aristotle speaks must be the
insistent claims of sense-perception, which he takes Parmenides
to have been unable to resist. From this passage it seems that
Aristotle took Parmenides to have placed the dictates of reason,

and those of organised sense-perception, in two water-tight com-
partments, between which there was no relation whatever, and
therefore no contradiction.

On this point Aristotle is the best guide we have, and it is
possible that he is right. Between a statement about that which is
and one about the world or ordinary experience there can be no
contradiction, because the latter is not false but strictly meaningless. That which is, is accessible to reason only and not to the
senses; the world of experience is accessible to the senses but not
to reason, in the sense that all statements about it are equally
meaningless, but sense-perception may give grounds not ration-
ally justifiable for preferring one such statement to another. The
position is perhaps tenable, though exceedingly uncomfortable,
as any position must be which makes an unbridgeable gulf between any two aspects of human experience. In considering this
total divorce between reality and appearance, it is impossible not
to be reminded of the Pythagorean separation of soul and body.
The machinery of the supernatural journey to another world,
seen from this point, appears a fit setting for the doctrines of
Parmenides.

The closer consideration of the cosmology of Parmenides
belongs to Chapter Seven.

The doctrines of Parmenides offend against common sense by
denying the reality of change and diversity. Since change can be
seen as a kind of diversity in time, the commonsense opponent of
Parmenides will wish to establish, above all, the existence of a
multiplicity of things, against the monolithic unity of Parmenides'
'that which is'. The arguments of Zeno, the fellow-citizen and
disciple of Parmenides, are directed against the possibility of any
multiplicity of things, or any movement. They depend partly
upon the ideas of Parmenides; but Zeno goes beyond his master
in the brilliant exploitation of difficulties inherent in the instinctive assumptions of common sense. There seems to be no reason
to doubt the account given in Plato's dialogue *Parmenides* (127D–
128E), according to which Zeno's arguments were designed to be

effective against anyone at all who might maintain the existence of a multiplicity of things. The evidence of Plato, Simplicius and the actual fragments shows that the standard form of a Zenonian argument was the deduction, from the premiss 'there are many things' (*polla esti*), of two mutually contradictory conclusions. Each argument would therefore reinforce the position of Parmenides, provided that Zeno's arguments were not mere copies of those used by Parmenides himself, and provided that they did not tend to undermine Parmenides as much as his opponents. Not all the arguments used were equally profound. Plato makes his Zeno explain that, as a whole, they were 'not a completely solemn performance', having been written with the aim of victory in philosophical debate by himself as a young man. This does not mean that individual arguments were not or are not important; in fact, the contrary is true.

Simplicius has preserved two arguments, one partly and one wholly in Zeno's own words. The former aimed to show that 'if there are many things, they are both small and large: so small as to have no size, so large as to be unlimited' (*apeira*).

The first limb of this conclusion was produced by an argument which Simplicius does not quote, but he says that it proceeded 'from the fact that each member of the plurality is self-identical and one'. The line of argument can be reconstructed with some probability. 'Many' involves a definite number of units—there cannot be any difference between 'many' and 'one' unless this is so. Then, each unit must be a genuine unit, must in fact be indivisible in any respect. Hence it cannot have size—which implies divisibility—any more than 'that which is' of Parmenides can.

The second limb of the argument is given in Zeno's own words. First, he argues that what is, has size. For suppose not: then there is something that is but has no size. Then: 'If it were added to another thing that is, it would make it no larger; for if it, being no size, is added, there can be no increase in size. This already shows that nothing was added. And if, when it is subtracted, the other thing that is is to be no smaller, nor is to increase when it is added, it is clear that *nothing* was added and *nothing* was subtracted' (fr. 2). But what can be described as 'nothing' is not something that is; hence what has no size, is not.

Since, then, what is has size, Zeno goes on to show that what has size is unlimited. 'But if it [a member of the plurality] is, then it must have some size and thickness, and one part of it must be at some distance from another part. Now the same reasoning applies to the former of these two parts; that too will have size, and so there will be a former [and a latter] part of it. If we can say this once, we can say it always, since there is no last term in the series, and it will never be that separation into two parts is impossible' (fr. 1). The conclusion follows immediately that what has size is 'unlimited'.

Every stage in this argument is full of interest. The various ideas that appear are the first statements of themes that run through the rest of Zeno's arguments and the whole of the history of philosophy as well. First, there is the realisation that there can be no disputes about 'one' and 'many', or in general about 'how many', unless there is an agreed answer to the question 'how many what?' There must be agreed units; but then the pluralists will be hard put to it to find anything that they themselves can agree to be a unit. To embarrass the pluralists with a superabundance of plurality is Zeno's favourite manoeuvre. Secondly, there are the special problems which arise if we assume generally (as most of Zeno's opponents must have done) that what is, is in space and time. In this argument, he explores the implications of 'size' (*megethos*), that is, spatial extension. His basic assumption, used in both limbs, is that what is spatially extended has two or more spatially distinct parts, which are themselves spatially extended. The assumption is effective *ad hominem* against most upholders of common sense, and most exponents of physics, since no remotely satisfactory physical theory has yet been advanced which does not make an assumption of this kind about the topology of space. Thirdly, the discovery of the infinite progression as a method of reasoning and arguing. Fourthly, the application of the infinite progression to generate series of entities in which there was, embarrassingly for his opponents, no last term; and in the exploitation of this embarrassment, the first exploration of the 'paradoxes of the infinite'. So, in this argument, Zeno draws the conclusion that anything that has size must be unlimitedly large, since it has an unlimited number of parts, each of which has size.

Four other arguments of which something is known fall recognisably within the same circle of ideas: two of the 'paradoxes of motion' recorded by Aristotle (those generally known as the 'stadium' and the 'Achilles' paradoxes) (*Physics* 233^a 21–3, 239^b 9–29); a general argument about plurality (fr. 3) preserved by Simplicius, and a further one mentioned by Plato as having been the first in Zeno's book.

The 'stadium' and the 'Achilles' employ an assumption about the divisibility of what is spatially extended similar to that stated above. As the arguments are phrased by Aristotle, they work in terms of points rather than of lengths, but this is unimportant. It is shown that in order to move any distance in a limited time, it is necessary to complete each one of an infinite series of movements. Thus, in the 'Achilles', the faster runner cannot catch the slower runner who starts ahead of him. For suppose them each to run at the same speed in a straight line all the time, let the slower runner start at the point T_0, and let him have reached the point T_{n+1} whenever the faster runner has reached T_n. Then it is easy to see that T_0, T_1, T_2, . . . and so on is an unending series of points, through each of which the faster runner has to pass before he catches up the slower. But to *complete* an unending series of movements, or of moments at which points are passed, is impossible; hence the faster runner cannot catch the slower, and in general nothing can move any distance.

A more general argument is that of fr. 3, preserved in its original form:

If there are many things, there must be just as many of them as there are, and neither more nor less. But if they are just as many as there are, they will be limited (*peperasmena*).

If there are many things, the things that are are unlimited (*apeira*).

For between the things that are there are always other things, and between these in turn other things, and so the things that are are unlimited.

In both limbs of this argument there is more than may appear at a first glance. In the first limb, the concept of the 'limit' (*peras*) as a mark of completeness is put to work in the same way as in Parmenides. If there are 'many things', they must come in units which can be counted. Whatever the number of the units, they must be as many as they are—the number must be 'up to specification', so that there is a *peras*, which is as much as to say that the number is a *definite* number. But a 'number with a limit' can also be understood as a *finite* number, and in order to produce a contradiction with the second limb, it is necessary to take it in this way too. In other words, this limb depends upon the belief, encapsulated here in the use of *peras* and its cognates, that what is definite is, necessarily, finite. Here again is a statement of a theme that runs through the whole history of philosophy: the attempts to get rid of infinites of all kinds as being undesirable, unknowable or unreal.

The second limb of fr. 3 depends upon the principle used by Parmenides (in section *B* of fr. 8) that any two things, to be distinct, must be separated by some third thing different from either of them. This may be given a spatial application or not (Zeno here uses the word 'between' (*metaxu*) of which the primary meaning is spatial). In any case, it generates, once more, an unending series of entities, for if A and B are separated by C, then A and C must be separated by D, A and D by E, and so on.

According to Plato, in his *Parmenides*, the first argument of Zeno's book stated that 'if there are many things, they must be both like and unlike'. It is easy to see how proofs might be constructed for these two limbs out of the same fund of general ideas.

There are four further arguments of Zeno of which something is known. The 'arrow' paradox, given by Aristotle (*Physics* 239ᵇ

5–9), had as its conclusion that 'a moving arrow stays in the same place'. It seems that Zeno argued: at every instant during its flight, the arrow occupies a space equal to itself, since no part of it can be in two different places at the same instant. But what occupies a space equal to itself is at rest. Hence the arrow is at rest at every instant during its flight. Hence it is at rest throughout its flight and so stays in the same place throughout. The paradox of the 'moving rows', again according to Aristotle (*Physics* 239ᵇ 33–240ᵃ 18), produced the conclusion that 'double the time is equal to half the time', and involved the assumption that a moving body with a constant velocity would take the same time to pass each of two other bodies of equal length, one stationary and one moving. It is not difficult to construct, with this assumption, the required result. Of the two others, one is an amusing puzzle (DK 29 A 24) about places: if everything that is, must be in a place then since a place is something that is a place is in a place, which in turn is in a place, and so *ad infinitum*. This clearly would be a useful counter to anyone who argued that 'that which is' must be in a place, which could not be identical with it. The other is an equally amusing and perhaps more profound difficulty (DK 29 A 29): if a certain quantity of grain, falling in a mass to the ground, makes a noise, then either there is a proportion between masses and noises, in which case even a single grain or the thousandth part of a grain will make a noise; or there is no proportion, in which case there must be a maximum number of grains which can fall together noiselessly, and it is necessary to suppose that the addition of the smallest fraction of a grain to this number will produce a noise. The interesting difficulty is, of course, not a problem about the behaviour of sound waves or auditory nerves, but an example of a general problem about the use of necessarily vague concepts.

It is not part of the purpose of this book to give a philosophical commentary on the arguments of Parmenides and Zeno. But the fact that those arguments persistently raise so many of the deepest and most permanent issues in philosophy is so striking that it requires at least some attempt at an explanation, which cannot but be coloured by a philosophical tinge.

What is clear is that Parmenides is making a conscious attempt at some kind of a new start. Like Descartes, he is trying to find an unassailable starting-point on which something further can be built. This search is understandable, given the intellectual situation of the time. The principles of the Milesians had yielded no one clearly true system, but a number of rival ones—in itself a scandal. Heraclitus had made the whole of cosmology suspect by revealing deep-seated contradictions at its heart. In the background, the Pythagoreans were directly or indirectly stimulating new lines of thought and using them, perhaps, for their own mysterious purposes.

In spite of the major problems of interpretation which have been left open, it is clear in what kind of way Parmenides makes his new start. His original alternatives, '(it) is' or '(it) is not', must on any possible interpretation be roughly equivalent to 'thought (about some subject) is possible' and its negation. If no thought is possible, we can do no more. But if it is possible, then something *is*, and we are therefore assured that 'that which is' is a subject of thought which will not produce contradictions. The next step is to examine what a thing's being implies. In order to avoid contradiction, it is necessary to reject anything that would allow the introduction of something that is not. This principle secures the elimination of all change and diversity whatsoever. Only one thing is, and that is perfectly and completely. It turns out that the assumptions of ordinary men and of cosmology are senseless, which surmounts the paradoxes of Heraclitus. Once the senselessness of these assumptions has been realised, they may safely be treated again as if they were a kind of truth, and systematised as far as possible. No contradictions can arise from this, for what is senseless can never contradict anything.

What is historically most important here is the logical analysis of such concepts as *time, change, diversity, separation, completeness*, all of them fundamental. Zeno's arguments continue the analysis, and reveal difficulties in making any of these concepts intelligible even for those who do not accept the general line of argument of Parmenides. Zeno's remarkable flair for argument could not have been called into play if Parmenides had not, with the originality of the pioneer, shown that the whole framework of ordinary human experience was open to question.

CHAPTER SIX

The Age of the Sophists

IN this chapter an attempt will be made to sketch the 'thought-world' of the intellectual movements in Greece between 450 and 400. Much will have to be abbreviated or left out altogether, and many difficult questions left undiscussed. In particular, the activities and influence of Socrates will be touched on only very briefly. The cosmological speculations of this period are reserved for the next chapter.

As a first approximation to an analysis of this complex and variegated half-century, it is useful to distinguish a negative, sceptical tendency, and a positive, humanistic one. The most characteristic products of the intellectual life of the period exemplify both of these tendencies, in various combinations, but they will now be taken separately.

The negative tendency, the scepticism of the age, owed much to the Eleatic philosophers. The arguments of Parmenides and Zeno administered a great shock to all established systems, and, beyond that, to all unconsidered confidence in the power of speculative reasoning, and further still. For their attack was upon what had seemed the indispensable framework of all thought, all knowledge, and all human experience. They appeared to have shown that the truths of reason were irreconcilable to the most ordinary assumptions of human life, and in particular to the assumption that sense-perception yields some kind of knowledge. Whether or not the Eleatic arguments could be blocked or circumvented, they had destroyed for ever any kind of instinctive confidence on these matters.

This destruction of confidence was the making of Greek philosophy. Much of what happened in the next hundred odd years—the most creative period of Greek philosophy and perhaps of all philosophy—can be understood as a prolonged struggle to come to terms with the Eleatics. But only the very first steps in the struggle are the concern of this book.

The direct influence of the Eleatics is evident in two works of this period of which we know something: the book of Melissus of Samos, and a collection of arguments by Gorgias of Leontini. Melissus, an odd and apparently uninfluential figure, was put down by Aristotle as a 'crude' thinker, and the fragments that survive do not make it easy to dissent from this judgment. For Melissus, what is is one and undivided, yet it is extended, infinitely, in both space and time. Of Gorgias of Leontini some more will be said later. In his collection of 'Eleatic' arguments, he argued in the style of Zeno to the conclusions: (*a*) that nothing is; (*b*) that if anything is, it cannot be known; (*c*) that if anything is that can be known, the knowledge cannot be communicated. This sounds like a *jeu d'esprit* designed to cast doubt on Eleatic ways of reasoning, but is likely to have had a didactic purpose as well or instead, for Gorgias was a professed teacher of the art of speaking—including that of reasoned argument.

From the arguments of Gorgias it is a short step to another, anonymous collection of arguments usually known as the *Dissoi Logoi* (Double Arguments). The purpose of the author is to show that it is possible to argue equally well on either side of any question, and he exhibits his skill or that of his teacher in treating various important topics. This again is probably a record of mental gymnastics designed for his pupils by a professor of the art of speaking.

Another person of this time who employed a technique of argument designed to produce scepticism was, of course, Socrates. The Socratic method was to question the proponent of any thesis about the meaning and consequences of that thesis, and by repeated questions to elicit contradictions and absurdities.

All such techniques are the expressions of the widely diffused though often ill-defined scepticism of this time. Protagoras of Abdera, the most characteristic figure of the age, expressed in set terms a relativistic view of knowledge which influenced most of his contemporaries. Against a radically sceptical view such as might be induced by the arguments of Zeno and Gorgias, the natural defence of common sense is to seek refuge in the certainty of immediate experience. This move then concentrates attention on the question of how much of the content of our experiences is genuinely public, how much private to the experiencing subject. Sceptical examination of this question immediately suggests a thoroughgoing relativism such as Protagoras, it seems, upheld.

Protagoras was generally influential, because he was the first figure of any distinction to express such a position, and he expressed it in memorable words. The beginning of his essay 'On the Gods' is characteristic:

Concerning the gods, I have no means of knowing either that they exist or that they do not exist, nor what sort of form they may have; there are many reasons why knowledge on this subject is not possible, owing to the lack of evidence and the shortness of human life (fr. 4).

His famous slogan, 'Man is the measure of all things' (DK 80 B 1) combined beautifully, as a good slogan should, the different components of his position: relativism or pragmatism in questions of truth, but also humanistic optimism about the problems of human conduct and society.

Protagoras was not a systematic thinker, and did not have a coherent theory of knowledge. His insistence on raw sensation as the basic datum and the test of truth was important, for all that, and provided the foundation for such attempts at a systematic empiricism as did occur. An interesting attempt of this kind is seen in the essay in the Hippocratic collection misleadingly entitled 'On Ancient Medicine'. The unknown author, who must have been writing very nearly at the end of the century, was a medical man who had heard and participated in contemporary debates on the theory of knowledge, and he exhibits some dialectical skill. The ultimate test, he insists, of whether a certain course of treatment or a certain regimen is good or bad is not whether or not it is in accord with some abstract theory, but how the patient himself feels. On this basis, the writer sketches a history and theory of medicine as a science that started from the ignorance of the primitive savage and has proceeded by purely inductive means towards a complete body of empirical knowledge about the effects on the human body of various treatments in various circumstances. It is an impressive programme, though the effect is spoilt when it turns out at the end of the essay that the writer himself holds certain theories about human physiology which could hardly be justified on his own principles. The so-called 'Epidemics', particularly Books I and III, the case-book of a physician practising in the northern Aegean, are another medical work of this period showing the same kind of influence.

More generally still, there was an empirical attitude in the air which made men sceptical of propositions which could not be supported by firm evidence. A favourite word in this context was *tekmērion*, 'grounds for belief'. So in the *Knights* of Aristophanes, a comedy produced in 424, the First Slave remarks fashionably to his colleague: 'Do you really believe in the gods? . . . On what *tekmērion* do you rely?' (*Knights*, 32–3). A quest for justification by the facts of experience cast doubt not merely on traditional and popular ideas about the gods, but on all speculation about anything at all remote. In 'On Ancient Medicine', the writer gives the nature of things in the sky and under the earth as examples of subjects on which it is impossible to speak with certainty: 'for there is no test, the application of which would give definite and certain knowledge'. In this too Socrates was in accord with the sceptical temper of his age; he abandoned or rejected cosmological speculation, betook himself to the study of man, and urged his listeners to do the same. In a significant passage Xenophon (*Memorabilia* IV 7) records the objections of Socrates to such speculation, and his arguments against the theory of Anaxagoras that the sun was a piece of rock which had been heated to a great temperature and had burst into flames. The arguments are good ones drawn from ordinary experience: for instance, that exposure to the sun makes the human skin browner, whereas exposure to an ordinary fire does not. (It should be added that Socrates, according to Xenophon, also had religious objections to physical speculation.)

It is not surprising, then, that while observations of heavenly bodies now began to be made in Greece with greater system and precision than ever before, the Milesian style of cosmology went out of fashion. Those who still tried to continue with cosmological speculation were bound to construct answers to the kind of objection outlined. The thinkers whose cosmologies will be described in the next chapter could be said to go 'beyond sense-perception' in two different ways: they produced sweeping theories about the history and workings of the *kosmos* and of the universe generally, and they also had theories about the ultimate structure of matter which were by no means obviously derived from experience. The general justification offered for both 'macroscopic' and 'microscopic' theories must have been the same: that men can learn about what is not immediately accessible to sense-perception by arguing from what is, as Anaxagoras put it in a fine slogan which cannot be rendered more shortly in English (*opsis tōn adēlōn ta phainomena*, fr. 21a); a principle implicit in all scientific work. This principle may have been used by Anaxagoras and the Atomists to justify even those arguments in their systems that would now be classed as 'logical', 'philosophical' or 'metaphysical' and which played a large part, as will be seen in the next chapter. That, in any case, there was always room for doubt, that all results were subject to revision in the light of fresh evidence, seems to have been realised, by Democritus at any rate, of whose remarks on the question a few are known. They are quoted, torn from all context, by a writer with a sceptical bias, Sextus Empiricus, and must therefore be treated with some care:

Anyone must realise, using this criterion, that he is remote from the real truth (fr. 6);

This argument again shows that in truth we know nothing about anything; what *seems* to anyone to be so is due merely to the impinging [of atoms] (fr. 7);

Yet it is clear that there is no way to know of what kind each thing is (fr. 8);

Truth lies in the depths (fr. 117);

What our mind grasps is in truth nothing reliable, but something subject to change according to the state of the body and of that which resists it (fr. 9).

The main theme of these remarks seems to be the unreliability of sense-perception. But Democritus, as might be expected, did not attack sense-perception in order to deny all possibility of knowledge. Instead, he set up as a standard a 'better' kind of knowledge than that afforded by sense-perception:

There are two forms of knowledge, one legitimate and one bastard. To the bastard kind belong all these: sight, hearing, smell, taste, touch. The other kind is legitimate and is distinct in nature from the former (fr. 11, part)

and Democritus apparently went on to say that while the bastard kind cannot discriminate things below a certain size, the legitimate kind is not subject to such limits. Clearly the 'legitimate kind' of knowledge is that derived from reasoned argument, as Democritus' own theories claimed to be derived. In just the same way, Anaxagoras recognised that the inability of the senses to discriminate things below a certain size made them only very approximate guides to the real structure of matter.

Both Anaxagoras and Democritus, then, were aware of the vagaries of sense-perception, but used them in a quite different way from Protagoras, in order to remove possible objections to their own theories based on general reasonings. Yet it remained true that the general theory of the structure of things advanced by either Anaxagoras or Democritus was dependent for its credibility on confirmation taken from sense-perception. The difficulty here, which is recurrent in the philosophy of science, was seen by Democritus, who dramatised the situation and represented the senses as protesting to the mind in a metaphor drawn from wrestling:

'Poor mind, you try to overthrow us using testimony which *we* supply! Our overthrow is your downfall' (fr. 125).

Besides trying to work out a coherent justification for his own theorising, Democritus counter-attacked Protagoras, with an argument that is also used in the *Dissoi Logoi* and by Plato: if Protagoras' thesis is that all propositions are only relatively true or false, then the thesis may be applied to itself, and hence there is a contradiction in supposing the thesis to be generally and absolutely true.

Democritus clearly took very seriously the problems sketched here, and it is unfortunate that so little of his ideas survives. From Theophrastus something is known of the elaborate detail in which he tried to work out the microscopic basis of sensible qualities, accounting for particular colours and tastes, for instance, as due to certain kinds of shape and certain combinations of atoms. A heightened awareness of the phenomena of perception and illusion was general at this time, and contributed to the raising of standards of evidence in all fields. The first and third books of the Hippocratic 'Epidemics' have already been mentioned; their author was always conscious of the need to record and preserve observations detached, as far as possible, from theory. The connections between this current in medical thought and the historian Thucydides are well established. The general ideas of Thucydides on history and society will be considered briefly later; here it is right to mention his deep interest, evidenced by many passages in his work, in the problems of truth and knowledge in history and generally, and particularly in the power and multiplicity of the illusions which distract men from reality, which are for him the most important pathogenic agents in human society. In his treatment of this topic he owes something to the medical writers, something to the Attic tragedians, but in the delicacy and penetration of his psychological analysis he is unequalled by any classical author.

The other characteristic, besides scepticism, of the outlook of this age was its humanism. At least in the earlier part of this half-century, though diminishingly so with the progress of the Peloponnesian War (431–403) there was a prevailing spirit of optimism about the human race and its capacity for wisdom, skill and social harmony. This spirit is expressed, for instance, by the well-known chorus in the *Antigone* of Sophocles (*Antigone* 332–75) and by the still better-known sculpture from the frieze of the Parthenon; both of these date from around 440. Periclean democracy was in charge of the Athenian empire, and the visual arts, and the Attic drama, were celebrating their conquests of the past half-century. This mood is that of the older generation of sophists: of Protagoras, Gorgias, and Hippias. It merged with the scepticism of the age to produce a cheerfully pragmatic attitude towards life, and a conviction that the proper study of mankind was man. The irreducible variety of human behaviour and character was accepted, and above all there was a faith in the ability of the human mind to surmount almost all obstacles by intelligence, especially when intelligence was accumulated and organised as a body of skill and knowledge, as a *technē*. The concept of *technē* had long been present in the Greek language, but at this time it was sharpened and made more significant. It came to suggest not simply a traditional skill or craft but a clearly articulated system of theoretical or practical knowledge, organised according to the nature of the subject—in other words, it took on much of the sense of the word 'science' at the present day. It is as professors of a newly self-conscious *technē*, the 'science of speaking', that the sophists must be seen.

It is necessary to add something here about the word 'sophist' (*sophistēs*). In the fifth century this word was still general in scope and neutral in tone: it could be used to denote anyone possessing exceptional knowledge, skill or talent of any kind, and was not necessarily derogatory or ironical. In the late fifth century it was applied not merely to the professors of speaking but to cosmologists, astronomers, mathematicians, and many others. Its later usage, down to the present time, was largely determined by the influence of Plato and Aristotle in the fourth century, who used it in opposition to 'philosopher', to denote someone who appeared to have philosophical ability and insight but in fact did not, and who gained his effects from fallacious argumentation not directed at the truth. It was natural that they should incline to see the fifth-century professors of speaking, as well as their fourth-century descendants, as 'sophists' in this sense.

It is now difficult to use the word 'sophist' in any precise sense, and in this chapter it has been and will be used as follows: 'The age of the sophists' means the period from 450 to 400, and 'the sophists' means the professors of the art of speaking who flourished during that period, and (sometimes) any other people who seem close to those professors in intellectual outlook and activities.

The professors of speaking professed to have reduced the use of language to a 'science', and offered to impart their knowledge for money to anyone. They are the first known exponents of the idea of 'higher education'. To anyone who could pay their fees, they offered mental training beyond what was required for ordinary life. It must not be concluded, though, that they proposed an ideal of mental culture as an end in itself. The notion of a purely intellectual (or for that matter aesthetic) way of life was not yet born, though it had been conceived; mental culture might be thought desirable 'in itself', but part of what would be meant by this would be that it made men more effective in social and political life. 'Education,' said someone perhaps of this period— meaning 'higher education'—'is a second sun to those who have it' (DK 22 B 134): in other words, it heightens the natural abilities and enables men to use them more fully and effectively. The older sophists would have agreed. Again, it must not be thought that there was any consciousness at this time of a difference between a training in speaking and a training in thinking. Rather, it was assumed that to learn to speak effectively is also to learn to think, and to apply thought, effectively.

The education offered by the older sophists was therefore strikingly like the traditional classical education of the English public school. Both were conceived of as a training for life, not for science or scholarship; both incorporated a humanistic and antidogmatic bias; both were purveyed principally to young men likely to fill positions of influence in public life; and both, further, were founded partly upon the study and interpretation of certain 'classical' authors, and partly upon the practice of speaking, reciting, and literary composition, all of which were taken to be disciplines aiding the development of the mental powers generally.

For such an ideal of education to be created and sustained, there must be striking personalities, partly scholars and wholly teachers, who command attention, if not respect, by what they are as much as by what they know. Such were the leading sophists of the older generation: Protagoras, Gorgias, and Hippias. Moreover, personalities need a stage. Most sophists were peripatetic, teaching wherever they could find pupils who would pay their fees; but they advertised themselves at such Panhellenic gatherings as the Olympic games, and as the century went on it was natural for them to congregate at Athens rather than elsewhere. Athens became an intellectual centre for a variety of reasons. With her maritime empire and commerce she was now the wealthiest Greek city and a natural centre of communications. The democracy, under Pericles, prided itself on its tolerance and openness to new ideas. The dramatic festivals were intellectual events unparalleled elsewhere in the Greek world. Later, under the severe strains of the Peloponnesian War, the boasted tolerance disappeared for a time. Three leading figures, Anaxagoras, Protagoras, and Socrates, were at different times prosecuted on charges of impiety or the like. Anaxagoras left Athens, where he had lived most of his life; so too did Protagoras, who gained the distinction of being the first man in history to have his writings burned by public authority. Socrates, who if he had wished could have escaped with exile or a large fine, chose to suffer the penalty of death.

Something has already been said about the figure of Protagoras of Abdera, who dominated the intellectual life of his time without being a truly original thinker. What he offered, as did Erasmus or Voltaire, was an original style of thought, an intellectual attitude. His writings expressed, memorably and with style, a spirit of irreverent detachment from accepted wisdom of any kind, and general scepticism about any broad assertions going beyond ordinary experience. Gorgias, of Leontini in Sicily, was above all the exponent of a new style of prose-writing, especially for public speaking. This style enjoyed a brief but intense popularity at some time before 400. Its characteristic feature is an elaboration of parallel and antithetic phrases and clauses in a continual striving after point and effect. Tedious and affected as it is, it must have seemed for a short moment to be *the* way to express thought in words. The illusion that it might be possible in this way to make language a true picture of thought took hold even upon powerful and independent minds like Thucydides, whose mature style still shows traces of the influence of Gorgias. The training in speaking and writing which Gorgias gave his pupils included also, as has been seen, some exercise in philosophical debate, though hardly for its own sake, but as a help to general dialectical skill. Hippias of Elis represents another aspect of the sophists—the ideal of encyclopaedic knowledge and universal skill. Hippias laid claim to some competence in geometry, geography, astronomy, literary and philological studies, painting and sculpture, besides public speaking and debate. Included among his interests was the history of thought, and he is the first person known to have interested himself in the earlier Presocratics as figures in that history.

The assumptions and methods of the sophists were attacked in the next century by Plato, whose criticism by its brilliance and power has influenced all subsequent estimates. But even in their own time the sophists will have had articulate opponents, most notably Socrates, whose method of discussion by question and answer is a way of dissociating two things that the sophists were prone to confuse: the force of reason and the power of the spoken word. So far as the sophists can be divided into an earlier and a later generation, the change between the two groups is intelligible as a response to criticism from Socrates and others; also, possibly, to the harsher realities of the Peloponnesian War. The later sophists have shed the comfortably tolerant and conservative assumptions of Protagoras and his contemporaries, and are driven to propound radical theories of morals and politics (about which a little will be said later). The difference is marked between

Plato's treatment of the other sophists, who are handled with
some affection and respect, even while their philosophical
shallowness and their minor faults of character are being revealed,
and his portrayal of members of the younger generation—such as
Polus in the *Gorgias* and Thrasymachus in the *Republic*—who
are shown as thoroughly unsympathetic.

The professors of speaking were not important solely as
educators. They laid the foundations, at least, of some theoretical
studies. The application of thought to the spoken word and its
effects on men produced the beginnings of systematic study of
the problem of meaning. Prodicus of Ceos, who belongs among
the older sophists, became known for his drawing of distinctions
of meaning between words commonly used as synonymous;
these distinctions were made by giving formal definitions of the
words in question. (The awareness of the need for clear and
general definitions in the scientific treatment of a subject is seen
also in the investigations of Socrates, and in the development of
geometry at this time.) Besides Prodicus, there are isolated reports
of further discussions foreshadowing those of the fourth century.
The interesting Cratylus, who has caused confusion in the study
of Heraclitus (see Chapter Three), and who influenced the young
Plato, held that change was so continuous and general in the
physical world that the only possible objects of reference in it
were the momentary states of objects, which could be referred to
only by pointing at the object at the moment in question. What
further objects of reference he admitted is not known, but he
seems to have held that there was or could be a single 'natural'
language in which everything had its 'real' name: a view not
surprising in a self-styled follower of Heraclitus. A more shadowy
figure is Lycophron, a sophist whose ideas Aristotle briefly
mentions. The problems about the nature of predication arise
naturally enough when one begins to think about language,
especially in the light of Parmenides. To say 'the man is white'
looks at first sight like saying that the man is identical with something labelled 'white', but a little thought shows that this must be

wrong, and that predication cannot possibly be identification of two things. Lycophron therefore proposed to drop the 'is' or its equivalent in such a statement, as misleading. We should say 'the man white' (this is not idiomatic in English, but the equivalent in Greek and in many other languages is). More importantly, Lycophron proposed to treat predications as assertions of the existence of a certain relation between the subject and the quality ascribed by the predicate—for example between the man and whiteness; this relation he termed 'togetherness' or 'coherence' (*sunousia*).

Thought about language also produced the beginnings of grammar and literary criticism. Poetry was studied for the first time as literature; instead of being simply amused, moved or instructed, men began to consider in a scientific spirit the means by which it produced such effects. The same study was given to the spoken word as an instrument of persuasion; mostly, of course, with application to politics and the law-courts, but not exclusively. The sophist Antiphon, according to one report, applied his science of persuasion to psychotherapy: 'He constructed a science of curing distress of mind (*technēn alupias*) analogous to the treatment of sick people by physicians, and having set up a room for the purpose next to the market-place at Corinth, he put out a notice saying that he was able to treat distress of mind by means of discourses. He would inquire the causes [of distress] from his patients, and then consoled them [sc. with his prepared speeches]. But he decided that this *technē* was beneath him, and turned to rhetoric instead . . .' (DK 87 A 6)

In all this there is the impetus towards making things systematic and explicit which can also be observed in the development of other sciences that attracted less public attention. It is this half-century that seems to have been decisive in the genesis of arithmetic, geometry and astronomy as sciences in their own right, with the recognition of the need for orderly arrangement, clear definitions, together (in mathematics) with explicit statements of assumptions and proofs, and (in astronomy) with accurate observations precisely correlated. At the same time there were attempts to systematise medical theory and clinical practice, athletic and military training, the theory of music and probably other branches of human activity as well. It is a search for defensible certainty in an atmosphere of scepticism. Thucydides reveals the origins of history as we now conceive of it when he tells how, at the onset of the Peloponnesian War, he decided to write the history of it, 'and I then lived through it all, being arrived at years of discretion and paying attention to things so that I might acquire some definite and certain knowledge' (v 26, 5).

The central topic of the sophistic age remained the same throughout: man, or the individual human being and the human race. In this chapter it is not possible to do justice to all the ideas about all aspects of human nature, history and society which sprang up like a tropical forest in these fifty years, and provided the timber out of which the great systematic achievements of the fourth century were constructed. Only a few of the more interesting lines of thought can be indicated briefly.

The study of human anatomy and physiology, in spite of the promising beginnings made earlier in the West (see Chapter Four), does not seem to have progressed much at this time. Accordingly, the best medical writers of the sophistic age are those who concentrate on summing up a great deal of clinical experience in practical treatises. It is the specifically human aspects of man that engage the attention of the best minds of this time: the variety and complexity of human emotion and motivation, man's adaptability to circumstances, his exceptional intelligence, and his unique social institutions, particularly language. This new emphasis is often associated with an optimistic view of human history as a continual slow progress, by a process of trial and error, towards a perfectly civilised life.

A much later writer, the historian Diodorus Siculus, has preserved an account of early human history which is certainly derived from a late fifth-century original. It is worth quoting in full. After a cosmogony in which the origin of the earth is explained, the account continues:

Then the earth first of all became more firm as the fire from the sun shone down on it; and then, when the warmth caused the surface to rise as if by leavening, some portions of moisture gathered together in many places on the surface and swelled up. In these swellings there formed putrid substances enclosed in fine membranes, as is still observed to happen in swamps and marshy places wherever the ground has been chilled and the air with a rapid change of temperature suddenly becomes blazing hot. These parcels of moisture, then, were impregnated with life by the heat in the way described, and while this went on they absorbed nourishment in the night-time directly from the moist that descended from the surrounding air, while by day they were made more solid by the heat. Finally, as the embryos attained their full growth, the membranes, shrivelled by heat, burst open, and there came forth animal forms of every kind.

Of these animals, those that had had the greatest share of warmth turned out winged, and took their way into the higher regions, while those in whose composition earth was prevalent were those classed as creeping things or land-animals, and those that had the principal share of moisture betook themselves to the appropriate place and formed the class of water-creatures. But as the earth was solidified more and more, by the sun's fire and by the winds, eventually it could no longer produce from itself any of the larger animals, and from then on each kind of living thing was produced by sexual intercourse.

Such is the account we receive of the first creation of everything, and they say that the first men to come into existence lived an unsettled and brutish life, going out to forage in ones and twos and eating the most agreeable of the plants and of the wild fruits. Attacks by wild beasts made them learn from expediency and come to one another's aid, and as they repeatedly gathered together from fear, they gradually came to know each other's features. Slowly they made articulate the utterances of their tongues, which at first were indistinct and unclear, and by making conventions among themselves about each object they taught themselves to use words to refer to everything. And because such groups formed all over the inhabited earth, not all men had the same language, because each group fixed its words arbitrarily. This is the reason why there are now all sorts of different languages, the first groups to form being the ancestors of all the different races of men.

Since no useful discoveries had yet been made, the first men had a hard life, without clothes or the use of fire or a settled habitation, and with no idea at all of the cultivation of plants for food. They did not even know how to harvest food that grew wild and store up fruits of wild plants for times of scarcity, so that many died in the winters from cold and hunger. But from this point on they learnt gradually from experience, and took refuge in caves in the winter and stored up such fruit as could be kept. Little by little fire and other useful things were discovered, and the various crafts (*technai*) followed together with other devices beneficial to civilised life. As a general rule, it was always necessity that taught men better, by giving appropriate instruction; and man received the instruction, being an animal who was naturally able and had, as his assistants in all he undertook, his hands, his reason, and his quickness of wit (Diodorus Siculus 1 7 and 8; Democritus, fr. 5).

It is disputed among scholars whether this account is due primarily to Anaxagoras or rather to Democritus, but for the purposes of this chapter it does not matter. One thing that is clear is that it draws on ideas going back to the sixth century: Anaximander gave essentially the same account of the origin of animals, and Xenophanes had the notion of gradual human progress by learning from trial and error. What is characteristic of the sophistic age is the special interest attached to the origins of language and society, and to the other characteristic features of the human species.

The lifelike depiction of human emotion in drama and the visual arts was, again, an achievement of the hundred years before 450. In the sophistic age what began to occupy the attention of sophists and dramatists alike was the complexity of human character and of human society, the possibilities for conflict between (for instance) reason and emotion in an individual, or between family ties and civic regulations, and so on. It was realised that the peculiar position of man among animals was connected in some way with the fact that he had a very complicated make-up, and human society equally. Sophists, with their practical interest in law-court speeches, were particularly interested in questions of guilt and responsibility, and the cases in which a human agent could claim to have been 'overcome' by some force so that the act in question was not truly his. But the greatest insight into the complexity of human motivation at this time is to be found in the Attic tragedians, and in the delicately clinical analyses of Thucydides.

The structure and functioning of human societies were often discussed in terms of an idea which had been current for about a century or more, but which underwent metamorphosis in this period. The analogy of Alcmaeon (see Chapter Four) between the human body and the 'body politic' presupposes a contrast between the natural action of the various 'powers' left to themselves, and the harmonising effect of the *krasis* that makes them an organic mixture. The beginnings of such a contrast can be traced back beyond Heraclitus to the poems of the Athenian lawgiver Solon in the early years of the sixth century, and it is also implicit in the cosmology of Anaximander, where the warring opposites are regulated and balanced by a Justice which is outside and over them. This contrast is one of the elements in the opposition between the terms *phusis* and *nomos*, which became a cliché in the later fifth century. Unfortunately the issues involved were confused by the inherent ambiguity of the word *nomos*. This word could mean not only 'law' of a necessary and non-arbitrary kind, but also simply 'custom', 'accepted usage', 'social convention'. Now it was again an observation of sixth-century Ionians that customs and social usages varied, often markedly, from one society to another. The effect of Protagorean relativism was to suggest that all such customs were equally valid, which was to say that they were all equally arbitrary. Here was a different *nomos-phusis* contrast, between 'arbitrary social convention' and the 'real state of things'. So Democritus explains his ontology by saying (fr. 9) that perceptible qualities, such as sweetness or colour, are only 'courtesy existents', of which the reality is a matter of convention, whereas what *really* exists is atoms and void.

Not merely were two logically quite different contrasts thus suggested by *nomos* and *phusis*, but there was a school of thought among the younger sophists that produced a theory-laden amalgam of the two. This school maintained that there was no 'natural law' in human society, and no natural and universal rules of conduct for the individual, so that all alleged 'laws' in these spheres must be mere arbitrary conventions, devised to regulate societies so as to protect the 'weak' from the 'strong'. To be 'natural', on this view, is to be completely selfish, because that is how men always behave when free from the artificial restraints of society. These extreme views are not characteristic of the older sophists, but seem to belong to the last twenty years or so of the century. A fragment of Antiphon, the only native Athenian sophist of any note, gives some idea of the tone and temper of the extremists:

. . . Justice, then, consists in not transgressing the laws and customs of the city of which one is a citizen. It follows that the way for a man to be just with most advantage to himself is for him to respect the laws when in the presence of witnesses, but when he is alone and unwitnessed to respect the commands of nature. What the laws command is an extraneous imposition; what nature commands is a constraint that is part of our very being. The law is an artificial convention, not a natural growth; but nature is natural, not conventional. If, then, you transgress the laws, you are free from shame and from penalty—provided that those who participate in the convention do not know, but not otherwise; whereas if you seek to repress, beyond the bounds of possibility, what inheres in your nature, the resulting damage to you cannot be any the less for being kept private, nor any the greater for being made public, because the damage is caused not by what people think but by what actually happens.

The point to which these considerations are leading is this: that *many duties imposed by law are hostile to nature.* Laws have been made for the eyes, to tell them what they shall and shall not see; for the ears, what they shall and shall not hear; for the tongue, what it shall and shall not say; for the hands, what they shall and shall not do; for the feet, where they shall and shall not go; and for the mind, what it shall and shall not desire. Can it really be that what the laws forbid men is no less repugnant and alien to nature than what they command?

. . . If, then, we consider rightly, it is not true that what is painful benefits nature more than what is pleasant; and it is not true either that what is in man's interest is the painful rather than the pleasant things. What is truly good for a man must benefit him, not damage him . . . (fr. 44, part).

There are famous statements of the same kind of theory in Plato's *Gorgias* and the first book of his *Republic*. But from essentially the same view of human nature it was possible to arrive at a utilitarian theory of moral and political behaviour, as is shown by what can be retrieved of the ideas of Democritus on this subject.

More significant here are the achievements of two Athenian citizens of the time, neither of them sophists: the historian Thucydides, and Socrates. No treatment of the sophistic age can well avoid returning again and again to Thucydides, who, by the time he reached the height of his powers at the end of the century, had subjected to scrutiny all the grand theses of the time, and rejected or interpreted them in the light of his independent and powerful intelligence. Thucydides saw human history as a great case-book of social pathology, and intended in his account of the Peloponnesian War to exhibit with accuracy and detachment the true course, the symptoms, and as far as possible the causes of that long sickness. In executing his design, he put into the mouths of representative speakers not merely what he took to be the determining considerations at crucial moments but much of his own view of man and society as well; in the speeches he is both showing by example how states work and analysing the examples and generalising from them. History was not to be written with the same intensity of concentration and rich intellectual resources for many centuries. No extracts from Thucydides will be given here, since a treatment that tried to do him justice would necessarily weigh down the balance of this chapter; adequate English translations are available, and the history requires to be read and reread as a whole.

Socrates, equally, cannot be properly discussed within the limits of this book. Being obsessed with the large problems about human conduct—how life should be lived and human acts appraised, what is the meaning of the key terms on which men rely in discussing such matters, 'good', 'bad', 'right', 'wrong', 'happiness' and so on—he applied to them a method of inquiry related to that of the newly developing science of geometry, characterised by an insistence on clear and general definitions and step-by-step reasoning from those definitions and what other assumptions might be available. But where the geometer's inquiries led him from theorem to theorem, or from problem to solution, those of Socrates led in general only from problem to problem, because of the inherent difficulty of the subject. And because his form of inquiry lent itself to dialogue, Socrates became a public destroyer of certainty about questions on which, instinctively, every man believes himself to have something worthwhile to say. It was the combination of this annihilating dialectical skill with the deep earnestness of the man that attracted and fascinated his disciples, including Plato; and through his influence on Plato's development Socrates became far more important for the history of subsequent philosophy than he can be proved to have been for the thought of his own lifetime.

CHAPTER SEVEN

Cosmology from Parmenides to Democritus

THIS chapter will handle that part of late fifth-century thought that was centred on cosmology and physics, and is therefore generally classed as 'Presocratic' rather than 'sophistic'. The distinction is convenient but in many ways artificial. Those who were interested in cosmology always had interests in common with those who were not. Yet at this time, as was explained in the last chapter, cosmological speculation had come to be thought of doubtful value by the most influential minds, so that those who still attempted such speculation were to that extent rather detached from the main currents of thought.

The cosmologists of this chapter fall into two classes. First, there are the 'Westerners', Parmenides and Empedocles, both familiar from earlier chapters, and whose cosmologies are distinctly outside the main Ionian tradition. Secondly, the later Ionians, of whom the most prominent are Anaxagoras of Clazomenae, Diogenes of Apollonia, and Leucippus and Democritus of Abdera. These men, all of them active, as it seems, between about 450 and 420, are recognisably attempting to continue the Milesian tradition in cosmology, with more or less regard for the criticisms of Heraclitus, Parmenides, Zeno and others. Nothing will be said here about the later fifth-century 'Pythagoreans' of South Italy. These interesting people kept alive a set of cosmological ideas which may have been genuinely Pythagorean. They later influenced Plato. But they were of small originality and depth, and remote from the important developments of the time.

I. PARMENIDES

It was argued in Chapter Five that Parmenides must have believed any cosmology whatever to be a collection of falsehoods, and that his own cosmology was merely intended to be the best possible in the sense that it systematised falsehood and accounted for the apparent facts in the most satisfactory way. How it was supposed to do this can be seen only to a very limited extent from the evidence available.

To begin with, it is clear that in a cosmology change and multiplicity must be possible. The minimal mistake, then, is to allow two subjects of discourse instead of one:

Mortal men, then, have settled their decision to name two forms, *one* of which they should not name—in this they have made a mistake —and separated them into opposite shapes, and laid down signs for them distinct the one set from the other: for one form, they have laid down flaming fire like the bright heaven, light and very rarefied, every way identical with itself, but not identical with the other; yet that other too they have laid down, as a separate thing, in opposition, as unknowing night, a dense and weighty body (fr. 8, 53–9).

It is emphasised here that this is not a matter of truth, but of a mistaken decision on the part of the 'mortal men'. Because it is a mistake to allow *two* forms instead of one, the giving of names to both of them is merely a matter of empty convention. Each of them must have not merely a name, but a set of characteristic predicates by which it is to be distinguished from the other; these too are supplied by arbitrary convention, thus:

Form I. Name: Fire; Predicates: light, rarefied, 'heavenly' (*aitherion*); Form II. Name: Night; Predicates: heavy, dense.

A further fragment continues from here:

But when once everything has received the names of *light* and *night*, and the predicates in accordance with their powers have been assigned to the various things, then all is full of light and obscure night together, the two in equal quantities, since what does not exist is not present in either (fr. 9).

The reasoning here is, as earlier in the poem, from lack of variance to symmetry. Light ('light' being another name of Form I), and night must be present in equal quantities, since there is no third factor to upset the symmetry between them. Clearly it is implied that this balance *always* holds, so that both 'forms' are subject to a law of conservation. Each of the forms, this fragment suggests, will inherit as far as possible the properties of 'that which is', being in itself unchanging, permanent and completely itself. Change and multiplicity will then have to be reduced to arrangements and rearrangements of the two forms. Aristotle (*Metaphysics* 986ᵇ 33–4) and the doxographers confirm this, though they call the two forms 'fire and earth' or 'hot and cold'; these names cast further light on the roles of the two in cosmogony, and Aristotle further tells us (*Metaphysics* 984ᵇ 1–8) that fire was the active, formative principle, and earth the passive one, making the pair analogous to the Yin and the Yang of Chinese thought.

More mysteriously, Aristotle says (*Metaphysics* 986ᵇ 34–987ᵃ 2) that Parmenides 'correlated' Form I with 'that which is' and Form II with 'that which is not'. One way of making something of this is to note that Form I, as fire and heat, is responsible for thought and intelligence, and 'that which is', in the earlier part of the poem, is also a thinking thing. Since Parmenides held, later in the cosmology, that perception is of like by like, this correlation suggests that a mind that became completely fiery would perceive only Form I, and therefore an unchanging and monistic world such as Parmenides himself believed in. The cosmology therefore, in a sense, incorporates the doctrines of the 'true way' and explains how true insight may be obtained. Something of the sort may hold good for Empedocles also.

Beyond this point, the evidence about the broad outline of Parmenides' cosmology is tantalisingly insufficient and puzzling. Among other interesting and unexplained features is a female goddess who is said to 'steer all things' and to 'initiate hateful childbirth and coupling', apparently through the power of love which she has created. It seems reasonable to think of this person in connection with the forces of Love and Strife in Empedocles.

The ideas of Parmenides in the special fields of astronomy and biology were briefly treated in Chapter Four.

II. EMPEDOCLES

The cosmic system of Empedocles was more discussed and quoted in antiquity than that of any other Presocratic. Aristotle considers and criticises it at some length, both Stoics and Neoplatonists were interested in it, and the poems of Empedocles survived till late in antiquity, enjoying some reputation as works of literature, so that the harvest of fragments is large.

Empedocles accepts at the outset the Eleatic thesis that what is cannot come into existence nor pass away. Accordingly he reduces all change, as Parmenides did, to the rearrangement of eternally persisting 'elements'. For Empedocles there are four of these, the 'classical' quartet of earth, water, air and fire, which had probably already been used by Heraclitus.

Alongside the four elements Empedocles introduces two further constituents, named Love and Strife, which are likewise eternal. They are supposed to occupy space, but it seems that they have no perceptible qualities of their own, and are detectable, if at all, by their effects on the neighbouring pieces of the four elements. For an understanding of the whole system it is essential to form a conception of what these effects were.

The importance of the concept of a *krasis* or 'duly proportioned mixture' in the medical thought of this time has been stated in Chapter Four, which also showed something of the community of interests between Alcmaeon, Parmenides and Empedocles in their medical and biological studies. Parmenides uses the word *krasis* in a fragment (fr. 16) about the physical basis of thought, and Empedocles, like Alcmaeon, certainly employs the concept and makes an implicit analogy between medicine and politics. In a *krasis*, disparate ingredients, each with its own proper qualities and methods of action on its surroundings, come together and are 'fused' in such a way that these private qualities and methods of action are effaced, and a uniform compound is formed with its own (perhaps quite different) qualities and effects. The fact that this is chemically possible was of course known from metallurgy, which also showed the necessity for proper proportioning of the ingredients. The application to organic systems seems to be a fifth-century Western Greek idea. In living things too, disparate components are joined in a unity that 'has a life of its own' overriding the private tendencies of those components. Something of this is in Heraclitus' *harmoniē*, but it is significant that Heraclitus chose mechanical examples, not organic ones.

It is the formation and maintenance of a *krasis* that, for Empedocles, is the primary effect of the presence of Love in things; and, contrariwise, Strife is above all the power that dissolves a *krasis* into constituents that war against each other. It is important to grasp this, for otherwise the cosmic system is unintelligible. The two powers act in this way on chemical compounds and organic systems and in social relationships, where households and larger communities are examples of more or less successful *krasis*, in which private interests are subordinated to the common good.

But the two forces do not merely prevail locally; Empedocles speaks of periods of alternate domination of Love and Strife in the *kosmos* as a whole. This suggests that the *kosmos* as a whole is, under Love, a huge *krasis*, and, in fact, so it turns out. When Love is in complete control, all the elements are fused uniformly throughout the *kosmos* to form a spherical deity who is one pure mind that does nothing but think, and is recognisably a descendant of 'that which is' in Parmenides. At the other extreme, the elements form no *krasis* at all with one another. This implies that they are all at war with one another, but not necessarily that they are spatially separated out to distinct areas of the *kosmos*. In between these extremes, whether they persist for some time or for a moment only, there are periods when Love is 'advancing' and Strife 'retreating', and conversely.

The world that we see is obviously not in a state of total *krasis*; on the other hand, there are many examples of local *krasis*, such as animals, plants, chemical compounds, and human societies.

It is clear we live in an epoch where pockets of Love and pockets of Strife are intermingled. Empedocles, in fact, believed that Strife was increasing at the time in which he lived.

This brief sketch leaves unanswered many questions. It is important to realise that Empedocles thinks of the *kosmos* as a whole as being always an organic system, except at the time of Strife's complete predominance, though it is, for most of the time, an incompletely integrated one. An analogy (fr. 20) which is in his mind here is that of the life history of a man, who begins from a seminal chaos, and through the stages of embryonic and juvenile development becomes steadily more articulated and coordinated, till he reaches the height of maturity, from which he declines, physically and mentally, until he can no longer function as a unity and dies. If this analogy may be pressed at all, the *kosmos* as such must have a mind, except in the period of 'total Strife', and must be organised in much the same way as an animal body in its constituent parts. There is nothing to contradict this supposition in the evidence, and some indirect support for it. For that 'everything has thought' is certainly an Empedoclean belief (fr. 110); and the analogy between the *kosmos* and the human body is worked out in a peculiar little work, 'On Sevens' (*peri hebdomadōn*), which cannot be much later than Empedocles and which shows some points of contact with what is known of Parmenides' cosmology.

It would be mistaken to ask whether the mode of action of Love and Strife is 'mechanical' or 'psychological'. It is mechanical in the sense that it seems to be invariable, the mere presence of Love or Strife in the neighbouhood of a piece of elemental matter being sufficient to make it respond in the appropriate way. It is psychological in the sense that everything has some kind of consciousness, and things are spoken of as acting 'by the promptings of Strife', as if Strife worked primarily upon that consciousness. Parmenides' goddess and her assistant Love may have worked in the same way.

Another causal factor in the *kosmos* of Empedocles, and one that seems to be independent of both Strife and Love, is the principle of the mutual attraction of similars, or 'like to like'. That birds of a feather flock together was proverbial already in Homer, and the application to cosmogony is found already in the congregation of the 'opposites' in Anaximander. There, however, it may be reducible to mechanical causes, which it certainly is not in Empedocles. Unlike Love and Strife, 'like to like' involves 'action at a distance' and seems to suggest a general 'cosmic sympathy' difficult to explain except in terms of sentient beings, which is possible for Empedocles.

The alternate prevalence of Love and Strife is treated as a fixed law of the universe admitting of no further explanation. Like the cosmology of Parmenides himself, that of Empedocles seems to be designed to allow the incorporation of Parmenides' 'true way'. For change and multiplicity are introduced into the *kosmos* only by Strife. Since perception is of like by like, the mind which has no Strife in itself, will not only itself function perfectly, but will perceive the *kosmos* as something free from Strife and under the sway of Love, in other words as a thinking unity like 'that which is'.

The cosmologies of Parmenides and Empedocles are, therefore, closely akin, as are those of their interests which were mentioned in Chapter Four. Their *kosmoi* are not pieces of a mechanism, but sentient organisms; biological ideas and analogies are everywhere apparent, as is also the wish to leave a corner for Parmenides' 'way of truth'.

III. ANAXAGORAS

Anaxagoras was a native of the small Ionian city of Clazomenae, where he was born (under Persian rule) at the beginning of the fifth century. He came to Athens in 480, presumably as a conscript in the army of Xerxes, and it seems likely that after the Persian defeat he settled there and lived there for some fifty years. At some time, probably around 430, he was prosecuted for impiety. One of the grounds of the charge was that he had stated the sun to be a large rock glowing with heat. Probably as a result of this prosecution, he retired to the city of Lampsacus, where he died. The prosecution may have had a political motive, for Anaxagoras was a friend of the statesman Pericles.

The cosmogony of Anaxagoras is like that of Anaximander in many points. A *kosmos* is produced by rotation, which causes separation-out of opposites, and of other things, from an original boundless and indeterminate mixture, by the agency of an all-powerful and intelligent deity. Many points of detail are also borrowed from the Milesians. Anaxagoras was clearly reworking the Milesian system of ideas. This involved clarifying what seemed confused, amending what seemed wrong, and supplying what seemed lacking, in the light of the new ideas of the intervening years. This process of adaptation may be traced in some detail.

Like Empedocles, Anaxagoras accepted without reserve the thesis that nothing that is can come to be or cease to be. Apparent cases of coming-to-be and ceasing-to-be were to be explained, therefore, as being really rearrangements of the ultimate unchanging constituents of things. This axiom made it impossible to be as vague as the Milesians, even Anaximenes, had been about the relations between the controlling deity, the original mixture and the emerging *kosmos*. Anaxagoras here broke sharply with the Milesian scheme, by making the controlling deity absolutely distinct from the *kosmos* and its components in the original mixture. Yet Empedocles, by making Love and Strife absolutely distinct from the four elements, had done much the same thing.

Some peculiar features of Anaxagoras' system seem to be due to his desire to circumvent the Eleatic arguments against plurality. Parmenides had argued (see Chapter Five) that any two things, to be distinct, must be separated or distinguished by some third thing; Zeno had accepted this premiss and derived an infinite progression; and, reversing the argument, he had claimed that any spatially extended thing must be divisible *ad infinitum*, and so not a unity, but an infinite aggregation. Anaxagoras, naturally, wanted a plurality of things, to account for the observed diversity of the world, so there would have to be a multiplicity of ultimate constituents. He then seems to have accepted Zeno's reasoning, and admitted that there would be an infinite progression. For Anaxagoras, then, there *was* an unlimited number of distinct ultimate constituents, and they *were* so arranged that between any two there was always a third. This clearly has the consequences (*a*) that there can be no lower limit of size for ultimate constituents; (*b*) that in any volume, however small, there may be an unlimited number of such constituents; (*c*) that there will be no clear boundaries, or at least no boundaries accessible to the human senses, between things.

That Anaxagoras did indeed reason thus and draw these consequences is strongly suggested by good evidence. The ultimate constituents are described as 'unlimited both in number and in smallness—even smallness turns out to be unlimited' (fr. 1). This is reaffirmed in fr. 3: 'There is no least in smallness, but there is always a smaller (since what is cannot not be); and in largeness there is always a larger. The large is equal to the small in number—considered in itself each thing is both great and small.' Here Anaxagoras recognises that infinite divisibility implies the absence of absolute units of length or volume, and hence the relativity of the terms 'large' and 'small'.

The next step is more surprising, though equally reasonable. Since things can be unlimitedly small, and human beings cannot perceive things below a certain limit of size, it is clear that a great deal of the structure of things must escape our direct observation. Below the limit of perceptibility there may be a great reservoir of variety, and hence of possibilities of change. Consideration of chemical and organic processes confirms this, as Anaxagoras realised, but he went even further, perhaps using the Zenonian idea that the ultimate constituents of things can have no boundaries among themselves without generating an infinite, dense series of other things. Anaxagoras advanced a kind of 'principle of maximum variety', expressed in the words: 'there is a portion of everything in everything', which has caused difficulties for his interpreters.

Symmetry requires that 'everything' should bear the same meaning in both occurrences. If so, 'everything' cannot be interpreted as 'every individual thing': for 'there is a portion of this chair in that table' makes no sense. The most natural course is therefore to suppose 'everything' to mean 'every kind of thing', where the 'kinds' in question are such things as gold, flesh, water, salt—whatever it may be that is named by each of the words 'gold', 'flesh' and so on. For this class of thing Aristotle felt the need of a technical name and used *homoeomeria*, but there is nothing to suggest that Anaxagoras used this or any other word in the same sense. Since there is no agreed modern word, it will be better to use a word like 'stuff' with no philosophical associations. Stuffs are entities which appear when we classify features of the world without relying on any notion of internal structure of dissimilar parts. Anaxagoras included among stuffs things like 'the hot' and 'the cold', that would not now be so thought of, and for some reason not entirely obvious he excluded earth, water, air and fire while Mind (*Nous*) had a special place. But, with these qualifications, 'a portion of everything in everything' meant 'every stuff contains a portion of every other stuff'—this is shown by the combined testimony of the fragments and of Aristotle.

Such a theory creates a reservoir of possibilities of change, as was said, and thereby avoids the kind of Eleatic objection that might have been brought against Empedocles' four-element theory. In Empedocles, a certain mystery remains about compounds, in which under the influence of Love the elements shed their usual physical properties, and acquire collective ones. Thus in Empedocles the elements can for a time 'lose their identity'; for Anaxagoras, as for a strict Eleatic, this is not possible. So whatever new properties emerge in rearrangements must have been there all the time. 'How,' asked Anaxagoras, referring to the facts of animal nutrition and reproduction, 'could hair come from what is not hair, and flesh from what is not flesh?' (fr. 10).

But the theory creates a variety far beyond what is needed to explain such facts, and was probably motivated by the Eleatic arguments mentioned above. This is also suggested by the difficulty of visualising the 'portions' (*moirai*). Consider any lump of some specific stuff X. It contains 'portions' of all other stuffs. What then makes it a lump of X, rather than of anything else? Anaxagoras had seen this difficulty, and proposed a rule of 'majority determination': 'a thing *is* that (stuff) of which it contains most'. This introduces the notion of definite quantities, which is difficult to explain. Within any lump of X, there is a 'portion' of Y. Either this 'portion' is present as a number of spatially continuous packets, or not. If not, then visualisation fails already and it is hard to see how talk of quantities is to be justified. But if the 'portion' of Y *is* present in spatially continuous packets within the X, there will presumably be 'portions' of X, and everything else, within the packets of Y, so that we are started on an infinite progression. This destroys the possibility of drawing any definite boundary between the X and the Y in the lump, be X and Y whichever ingredients they may, and this in turn destroys the notion of a packet with which the infinite progression started. For this reason it seems necessary to suppose that Anaxagoras, moved by Eleatic reasoning, deliberately tried to abolish the notion of a definite boundary between any two ultimate constituents, and hence that the 'portions' are not to be understood as spatially continuous packets. This is confirmed by the fragments. 'No one thing can be distinctly separate from another, but all things have a portion of everything . . . no distinct separation is possible, nor can something come to be by itself' (fr. 6, part). 'Nothing is absolutely separated out or distinguished from another thing, except for Mind . . .' (fr. 12, part). 'The things in the one *kosmos* are not distinctly separated from one another, nor are they chopped asunder by the axe . . .' (fr. 8, part). So the 'portions' must be thought of as proportions that cannot be directly located or directly measured. The internal structure of material things remains, as in Empedocles, essentially mysterious, though indirect inferences can be made by observing the behaviour of stuffs in chemical and other changes. 'The quantity of the things that are separated out cannot be known either by reasoning or by practical measures' (fr. 7). Both Empedocles and Anaxagoras constructed theories of the microscopic structure of matter that

took account of the observed facts known to them, but left too
much irreducibly inexplicable.

The doctrine of Mind, like that of the 'portions', is so contrived as to satisfy both metaphysical and cosmological requirements. Mind (*Nous*) is recognisably a descendant of the Milesian
deities; it is all-powerful and omniscient, and orders the *kosmos*
or *kosmoi* according to a plan. It is described in one of the fragments, in stately prose with a religious colouring:

> While all other things contain a portion of everything, Mind is
> unlimited and independent and is not mixed with anything, but alone
> exists by itself. For were it not by itself, but mixed with something
> else, it would contain a part of all things by being mixed with one
> thing, since, as I have already said, there is a portion of everything in
> everything. Moreover, the things that were mingled with it would
> prevent it from controlling anything to the extent that it in fact does
> control everything, being unmixed. For it is the subtlest and purest of
> all things; it also possesses all knowledge about everything, and is of
> the greatest strength. All living things, both great and small, are
> controlled by Mind. The whole of the rotation was ordained by the
> controlling power of Mind, which ordained that there should be a
> rotation in the first place. First the rotation began over some small
> region, but it spreads now over a greater area, and will spread over a
> yet greater. The things that become mingled and those that become
> separated out from the mixture and distinguished from one another—
> all these are determined by Mind; and the kinds of thing that were to be
> and that once were but now are not, and all that now is and the kinds
> of thing that will be—all these are disposed by the ordering of Mind.
> So too was this rotation that is now made by the stars and the sun and
> the moon and the *aēr* and *aethēr* that are being separated out from the
> mixture . . . (fr. 12, part).

Much of this could have been said by Anaximander or Anaximenes, with a few obvious substitutions. The deepest difference
is that which is marked by the choice of the name 'Mind' (*Nous*)
for the supreme power. The *nous* or *noos* in early Greek is that
part of the man which is responsible for the intelligent apprehen-

sion and judgment of the world around him; it is not at all a source of action. The Milesians had thought of the divine power in the universe as like the *psuchē* in the body. In substituting 'Mind' for *psuchē*, Anaxagoras shows that he has discarded this analogy in favour of another one: that of the mind's creative and ordering power in the realm of pure thought. In other words, the universe, or at least the *kosmos* or *kosmoi*, are to be thought of as like the ideas in God's mind, not the body which God inhabits.

This change of analogy had of course been prepared by the previous development of thought. In Heraclitus it is difficult to tell how far the designs in God's mind are distinguished from the execution in the world, or indeed how far God's mind is distinguished from the world. The arguments of Parmenides seemed to show that all reality must indeed be a mind, or an object of thought in a mind. Anaxagoras, therefore, in making God a mind and the world, in effect, his thought, avoided the uneasy ambiguities of Heraclitus and could accept the Eleatic principle that whatever is is an object of thought, and conversely. It has been seen that in attempting to accommodate other Eleatic arguments, Anaxagoras had been driven to a theory of the micro-structure of matter which made it, to some extent, mysterious to human reason. The fact that the whole disposition of matter was determined by Mind did at least guarantee the ultimate intelligibility of the whole, and this accounts for the emphasis on the fact that it was '*all* determined by Mind'.

Not only the ultimate intelligibility, but the ultimate purposefulness and fitness of the whole plan is suggested by Anaxagoras' words; it seems likely that he stated explicitly that it was the best possible plan, and that all God's work was for the best. It was this suggestion that excited the interest of Plato and Aristotle in Anaxagoras, and their complaints (Plato, *Phaedo* 97B–99C; Aristotle, *Metaphysics* 985^a 18–21) that he nevertheless explained particular features of the world by 'mechanical' causation point to a crucial difficulty. The fragments do not explain, and to judge from what Plato and Aristotle say, it was nowhere explained what the relations and the division of responsibility were between

the superintending Mind and the mechanical causes that undoubtedly operated in the *kosmos*. In particular it is not clear
whether the mechanical causation was thought of as something
inherent in the nature of matter, and therefore not created but
only used by Mind—if so, then Mind's role is much like that of
the Demiurge in Plato's *Timaeus*—or whether Mind created the
'lower-level physical laws' as part of its plan. The first alternative
seems the more likely, for the assumption always was that stuffs
like water and fire, to say nothing of 'the hot' and 'the cold', had
inherent physical properties that acted upon their surroundings.

If this is right, Mind does not intervene in the working of the
kosmos at any particular time, except perhaps at the beginning.
The whole history of the *kosmos* from that beginning onwards
was planned by it beforehand, and proceeds like a premeditated
human action successfully carried out. This takes some of the
edge off Eleatic criticisms of change, since any future state of the
world is in some sense already present in Mind.

One interesting question that remains is that of the relation
between Mind and the intellectual faculties of men, and of animals
generally. The evidence is that 'mind' in men was identified with
Mind, and that all other animals also contained 'pieces of Mind'.
This comforting doctrine has some paradoxical consequences.
Since Mind is impassive and unmixed, its functioning is never
impeded; so what I misleadingly call 'my' mind—it is not 'mine'
in any real sense—never makes a mistake, and is omniscient. If
the same is not true of me, it must be because I am somehow not
sufficiently receptive of what Mind tells me—but what part of me
could be receptive, except my mind? The only way out of this
kind of difficulty would seem to be to suppose that each portion
of mind functions, not as Mind as a whole does, but like a Leib-
nizian monad, reflecting the world from a particular point of
view.

In any case, if Mind is the standard of goodness as of reality,
the 'best' man will be the most purely intellectual, and the most
remote from the world of the senses and of action. Some confirmation here is given by anecdotes related by Aristotle (DK 59 A 30),

according to which Anaxagoras said that the most happy man was someone who would seem a strange person to the common run of men, and that what made existence as a human being preferable to non-existence was the possibility of contemplating the universe.

An account has been given of the most characteristic general features of Anaxagoras' system. The details of his cosmogony and cosmology are, by comparison, of less interest, and do not show any evidence of greater insight into the mechanisms of the world than the Milesians already possessed. The account of human history and progress relayed by the historian Diodorus Siculus (see Chapter Six) which seems to be derived from Anaxagoras, suggests that he here reworked earlier (Milesian) ideas, with a keen interest, typical of his age, in the distinguishing characteristics of the human race and their origin.

Anaxagoras had a sensitive and subtle mind, fertile but not analytic. He did not meet the Eleatic arguments face to face, but attempted to construct a system that would save cosmology at least from the most damaging criticisms. His solution remains intrinsically interesting, in contrast to such systems as that of his younger contemporary Diogenes of Apollonia, who does not seem to have attempted original thought, except in details of cosmology and physiology, and whose general level of philosophical awareness suggests the age of Anaximenes, not that of Anaxagoras and the sophists.

IV. THE ATOMISTS: LEUCIPPUS AND DEMOCRITUS

Of the life of Leucippus we know next to nothing, and there is little trustworthy information about that of Democritus. Both were citizens of Abdera, a small city on the northern shores of the Aegean, which like Elea had been founded by refugees from old Ionia. Democritus was perhaps the younger and, born like Socrates around 470, he lived on well into the fourth century.

Leucippus and Democritus were responsible for the Atomistic

theory. Even though they were contemporaries of Socrates, their speculations are traditionally and reasonably grouped under the heading 'Presocratic', for the Atomistic theory is the last and greatest original effort in that kind of physical speculation which originated with the Milesians. The respective shares of Leucippus and Democritus in its creation cannot be certainly defined, but it seems likely that the leading ideas of the theory were due to Leucippus, and that Democritus, a more prolific and many-sided but less original thinker, worked out the applications in greater detail. There are a few inessential points on which the opinions of the two are said to have differed, but it is not possible to prove disagreement on any fundamental question.

The starting-point for the Atomists, as for Anaxagoras, was the effort to find a way of reconciling the Eleatic arguments, so far as they were taken to be valid, with the construction of a cosmology that accounted for the perceptible world. But while Anaxagoras tried to create a multiplicity without definite units, the Atomists took very seriously the need for indisputable and absolute units of whatever existed, and therefore collided with Parmenides and Zeno at a different set of points.

Zeno had argued that two things that are can be distinguished into two units only by means of some third thing 'between' them, that must itself be; and thence arises an infinite progression. For this reason, Leucippus, according to Aristotle (*de Gen. et Corr.* 325ᵃ 23–9; *Metaphysics* 985ᵇ 4–10), took a drastic step: he proposed to introduce 'that which is not' (*to mē on*) as a factor in the explanation of the world, and so to assert (it would seem) that it somehow *was*. As Aristotle puts it, the proposal of Leucippus is unintelligible because it is so blatantly self-contradictory; but there are good reasons for thinking that Aristotle is mistaken. For another remark, by Democritus, says, not that 'the non-existent exists just as much as the existent', but that 'the "nothing" exists just as much as the "thing" '. Here the words translated by 'the "nothing" ' are '*to mēden*', 'that which is nothing', and the words translated by 'the "thing" ' are '*to den*', where '*den*' is a nonce-word, formed from '*mēden*' by the removal of the negative prefix '*mē-*'. The point of this linguistic joke must be that '*to mēden*' is *not* to be taken, as Aristotle wrongly takes it, as equivalent to 'the non-existent', since what is not *to mēden* is not *to on* but *to den*. The point that Democritus seems to be indicating is that 'nothingness' is just as real as any 'thing', but differs in not being a 'thing', or, as one might say, not being an individual or a primary object of reference, though to say this is to import a higher level of sophistication than was available at the time. How does this distinction help to answer Zeno? If 'things' are separated by 'the nothing', what separates or distinguishes 'the nothing' from any 'thing'? There are no reports on what the Atomists replied or would have replied to this question, but it seems that consistently with their position they had just one convincing answer. Qualitatively, 'the nothing' is distinguished from any 'thing' simply by lack of 'thingness', by not being an individual with all that that implies. Spatially, there is no further entity required to divide 'nothing' from any 'thing'. For though there must be a *boundary*, this can perfectly well be *part* of the 'thing'. This kind of question about the topology of space was later treated elaborately by Aristotle, but it must be admitted that he gives no hint that the Atomists had contributed anything to the debate. Some indication that Democritus was interested in these questions is given by a puzzle of his preserved by a later writer (DK 68 B 155). The substance of it is this: suppose on a line there can be two points 'next to' one another with no intervening point. Then let a right cone be intersected by a plane parallel to its base and passing through the point on its axis which is 'next above' the point where the axis meets the base. Will the circle of intersection be smaller than or equal to the base? Clearly either answer leads to absurd results, which shows that two points on a line cannot be 'next to' one another in this way. It is interesting that Democritus should be arguing like this since the density of points on a line is crucial for the suggested answer to Zeno. If points on a line were not dense, then one could ask what separated the last point in a 'thing' from the first point in 'the nothing', and there would be no plausible answer.

Once 'the nothing' was admitted, it could perform two functions: it separated 'things' from one another, and so made a
plurality possible, and it allowed change of place by things, so
making possible all change which could be reduced to rearrangements of unit 'things'. 'The nothing' therefore functioned as
'empty space', or 'void', and the sources usually call it 'the void'
(*to kenon*). It was the first time that a well-thought out concept of
a purely passive and empty space had been propounded, though
it may well be that the mysterious 'Pythagoreans', of whose
opinions Aristotle tells (see Chapter Four) had hit upon the idea
of a unit-separating void before the Atomists did. Though con-
demned in ancient times by the high authority of Aristotle, and
in modern times by many influential thinkers, the notion of a
purely passive space has a way of persisting and of making itself
indispensable to physics; so its introduction by the Atomists is a
noteworthy landmark.

The 'things', the units that moved about in, and were separated
by, 'the nothing', were to be indisputably *units*; so each of them
was uncreated and imperishable, and could not be divided,
whence the name *atomon*, 'indivisible thing'. Each atom was in
fact the heir to many properties of Parmenides' 'that which is'.
But not to all; most obviously, the atoms were in space, and
might be of any shape.

Some confusion has existed ever since the time of Aristotle
over the question whether the atoms were 'mathematically' or
'theoretically' as well as physically indivisible. The problem
arises in this way: it is clear from many pieces of evidence that the
atoms were thought of as spatially extended and as having
various shapes, which could (for instance) cause them to inter-
lock, and as possessing weight in proportion to their volume.
They could vary in size, and according to one (late) witness
Democritus imposed no upper limit of size on his atoms. Not all
of the evidence available is totally reliable; there are some contradictions, and a suspicion that the doxographic tradition has
been infected by the misrepresentations of an Epicurean writer.
Nevertheless, it is clear that the atoms were spatially extended,

three-dimensional objects. Any such object can be said to be 'theoretically' divisible, in the sense that one can always distinguish, at least in thought, as Zeno had pointed out, two or more distinct and spatially separate three-dimensional regions within it—that is to say, this is possible if one accepts ordinary ideas about the local topological structure of space, and in particular those assumptions about that structure which are enshrined in Euclidean geometry.

The Atomists, then, were in a dilemma. Either they had to deny that atoms were 'theoretically' divisible, which in turn meant either overturning ordinary notions of space or refusing size and shape to atoms; or they had to allow 'theoretical' divisibility and thereby to fall foul of the arguments of Zeno, that what was even 'theoretically' divisible had ceased to be a true unit and contained infinitely many sub-units. Since it is clear that atoms did have size, and almost certain that no innovations were made in ordinary notions of space by the Atomists, it would seem to follow that atoms must have been 'theoretically' divisible. The difficulty is that Aristotle, who would be expected to be the most competent witness, speaks in a way that seems to mean that the atoms were not 'theoretically' divisible. Aristotle, however, had his own theory about the relationship between 'theoretical' and 'physical' divisibility, and it is likely that he did not prevent his private assumptions from colouring the account he gave of the Atomists. The doxographical evidence is self-contradictory and of doubtful value.

It is necessary, therefore, to suppose that the Atomists acknowledged the 'theoretical' divisibility of the atoms while denying their physical divisibility. The problems discovered by Zeno about space and change would still, of course, remain, and how the Atomists proposed to deal with them is not known.

The atoms, then, were spatially extended and physically indivisible. They were also unlimited in number, unchanging in shape, size and internal structure, and they moved for ever in a limitless void. The Atomists now had the task of accounting for the observed structure of the world and the contents of personal experience on these economical foundations.

It is natural to begin by asking about the ways in which the atoms moved. The evidence is conflicting and there may have been deliberate distortion by Epicurean sources. Aristotle, so far as he goes, is the most reliable witness. His testimony (DK 68 A 37) seems to show that the atoms had no inherent tendency to move, and that there was not (as there was in Epicurus' universe) an absolute 'upwards' or 'downwards'—the void was symmetrical in every respect. Accordingly, atoms moved only because impelled by the impact of other atoms. They were said to have weight in proportion to their size, and weight could be explained in terms of resistance to impact. Whether an atom, if undisturbed, was thought to continue in its state of motion indefinitely or gradually to come to rest, is not clear.

Within a *kosmos* other dynamical principles were thought to apply, of which the justification in terms of collisions of atoms is not obvious. Heavier atoms were more drawn towards the centre than light atoms, and there was also a tendency for atoms of like size and shape to congregate together. Democritus appealed (fr. 164), in support of this principle, to the analogy provided by the arrangements of pebbles of various configurations on a sea-shore. It is likely that this kind of analogy was the most that could be offered by the Atomists to make plausible some of the steps postulated in the creation of *kosmoi* from atoms and void. There is no sign that they made any real advance towards a systematic treatment of dynamics, much less a mathematical one.

For this reason, the cosmological devices used by the Atomists to explain the creation and working of *kosmoi* do not differ much from those well-established in the Presocratic tradition. They give the impression of being artificially pasted on to the new metaphysical foundations. The formation of a *kosmos* was roughly as follows. A chance and sudden congregation of atoms of the same order of size in a relatively crowded space caused a rotatory movement to occur. This may have been supported by analogies in observed facts: vortices are observed to form in water when it runs out of a large vessel through a narrow passage. What was further required, then, was a way of shutting atoms in from the rest of the universe. This was done by supposing the formation by random movements of a 'fence' of interlocked atoms. In favour of this step, it can at least be said that there would be a kind of 'natural selection' at work; atoms once interlocked would stay interlocked unless subject to exceptionally strong and well-directed blows from outside. The principle of 'like to like' would guarantee that 'fences', once in existence, would tend to extend themselves, and that the atoms shut into any *kosmos* were all of more or the less the same size, a point important for the theory of perception.

Once the rotation had begun, the cosmogony proceeded on familiar lines. By a process of segration by weight, the four elements—which were explained by four particularly natural and stable kinds of 'molecule'—are created and sorted into the usual arrangement, and function thereafter in traditional fashion. Traditional also was the possibility of the existence of an unlimited number of *kosmoi* simultaneously in different parts of the void; possibly new was the idea that the collapse of a *kosmos*, which occurred eventually upon excessive pressure from outside, left 'ruins' which often furnished material for a new *kosmos*.

In one respect the system of the Atomists was revolutionary. All their predecessors had asserted, either explicitly or implicitly, that the intelligibility and rationality of the universe depended ultimately upon its subjection to a divine power which in some sense was conscious and intelligent. The earliest thinkers had no doubt said rather little about the nature and purposes of the deity. Heraclitus and Anaxagoras had said more. Even in Parmenides, 'that which is' is a timeless unified thought; and the same is true, with some qualification, for the 'Sphere of Love' in Empedocles. It is true that the Sphere comes to be only intermittently; yet because 'everything has thought and a share of intelligence', it is always potentially present in the scattered thoughts of the various particles of matter. The Atomists went counter to the whole tradition by removing everything 'mental' from the list of ultimate constituents, a noteworthy act which must be examined more closely.

The reduction of everything to atoms and 'void' did not by itself entail the denial of an ultimate 'mental' constituent, for it would have been possible to suppose that each atom was a mind—again, a suggestion of Leibniz's monads. But such minds would have had to be timeless, since the internal structure of atoms could not be allowed to change in time; and therefore would not have been able to play any part, as minds, in the determination of events in the universe. The inner logic of the Atomist theory, therefore, led straight to the conclusion that consciousness and perception, as they are known in ordinary experiences, are epiphenomena, determined and accounted for completely by the states and rearrangements of components not themselves capable of consciousness or perception. (It is for this reason that Democritus has to say that perceptible qualities exist 'by courtesy' only (see Chapter Six).) It followed that the whole history of the universe was determined, if at all, by a 'meaningless' necessity inherent in the laws governing the collision and rebound of atoms, a force which was devoid of any inherent tendency to the better, or of any regard for the wishes and requirements of such accidental by-products as conscious beings. Democritus conceded, indeed, that 'gods' might exist; but by 'gods' he meant only conscious beings which were created and perishable, though noticeably superior to human beings in size, beauty, strength, intelligence and moral qualities.

The last and greatest representative of the Milesian tradition, therefore, was the first explicit materialist. It would be wrong to conclude from this that materialism had been 'in' the tradition all along. Anaxagoras' system represents another equally possible line of development. Neither of these lines was to be taken any further, however, for a long time. The sophistic age had undermined the whole tradition of cosmology, and when in the fourth century cosmological ideas began again to be discussed, the dominant minds, shaped in the fire of philosophical debate, gave them a different turn and subordinated them to other considerations.

CHAPTER EIGHT

Conclusion: the Study of the Presocratics

FROM what has been said in earlier chapters, it should be clear that in the study of the Presocratics the handling of the evidence is peculiarly difficult. The sources available in modern times from which knowledge of these thinkers can be drawn, consist of such accounts of their thoughts and such quotations from their works as occur in those writings of classical antiquity which have been preserved. Not one of the more important figures with which this book is concerned (except for Thucydides) can be known to us with the directness and fullness which the survival of a complete text makes possible. Instead, it is necessary to look to scattered fragments of the original works, quoted usually without indication of the context, and to a number of second-, third- or fourth-hand accounts of the contents of those works, each of which has been subject to a number of influences causing unconscious or deliberate distortion of the truth.

This being so, an introduction to the Presocratics cannot be complete without some sketch of the main sources and the problems connected with them. The chief purpose of this chapter is to give such a sketch.

In Chapter Six, the sophist Hippias of Elis was said to be the first person known to have concerned himself with the history of thought. Little trace remains of his activities in this field, and it is only in the fourth century that such studies begin in earnest, in the philosophical schools of Plato and Aristotle.

Plato, as the disciple of Socrates and the associate of Cratylus, was from the beginning sceptical of the possibility and value of cosmology, and as his own ideas developed they led him further and further away from the study of the world as it presents itself to sense-perception. Yet his vision of a universe ruled by mathematical truths drove him to write the *Timaeus,* which owes a great deal to the 'Pythagoreans' of the later fifth century, and generally to the 'Western' tradition of cosmology, biology and medicine. But in general Plato is interested in the Presocratics only so far as they can be plausibly interpreted as metaphysicians. Heraclitus appears in Cratylus' version; Parmenides and Zeno, naturally, are particularly praised and admired. In one passage (*Sophist* 242C–243A) Plato even suggests that all the Presocratics were really metaphysicians, who wrapped up their ontologies in the dress of cosmologies. The suggestion is thrown out in passing, and may be not meant seriously; but it shows how a growing philosophical sophistication leads almost inevitably to distorted views about the previous history of thought. Plato himself was old enough and wise enough not to be carried away; but some of his less critically-minded pupils seem to have tried to show that Pythagoras, for instance, founded a school on the lines of Plato's Academy. It may be, too, that the arrangement of the Presocratics into two or more 'schools', with regular descents from teacher to pupil, derives from the same passage of the *Sophist*. Another notion reinforced by Plato's authority was that Egypt was the source of all genuinely ancient wisdom, a notion reflected in the feeble 'biographies' of early philosophers which were composed not much later.

It is to Aristotle, more than to any other man, that we owe the survival of a certain quantity of reliable information about the Presocratics. This fact is explained by his theory of scientific method. In all the 'sciences'—under which term Aristotle comprehends all branches of philosophy as well as mathematics and the natural and social sciences—the correct method of investigation involves taking account of certain items given in experience, and these include the opinions of previous authorities on the subject. For the proper investigation of physics and metaphysics, therefore, it is necessary to take into account, and therefore to know, the opinions of the Presocratic cosmologists, and the arguments of Parmenides and Zeno.

For this reason, the surviving works of Aristotle contain much information about the Presocratics. Directly, and through his pupil Theophrastus (to be discussed presently), he set a pattern of interpretation of these thinkers which, though it can be shown with more or less probability to be inadequate or mistaken at certain points, is hard to replace because it is the pattern within which almost all the rest of the evidence, apart from verbatim quotations, is set. This pattern is derived from Aristotelian doctrines about the physical world; the Presocratics are seen as men groping their way towards these doctrines. Where possible, their ideas are interpreted in Aristotelian terms; where this is clearly not possible, Aristotle may dismiss them as 'confused'. It is, of course, true that the thought of the Presocratics is far less well articulated than that of Aristotle. It does not follow that they did not have important un-Aristotelian things to say. Aristotle, in fact, provides many examples of the kinds of mistake that menace every serious attempt at a history of thought. One is the mistake of simple anachronism in interpretation; another that of giving a false impression of inevitability, as if the thinkers in question were a disciplined army marching towards the objective of 'modern thought'; and yet another is that of being betrayed by philosophical prejudices into an unjust and uncritical treatment.

Aristotle is not free from these mistakes. In spite of that he is honest and scholarly when he makes specific statements about particular thinkers. (His generalisations are rather less reliable.) His comments on the Presocratics are the best-informed and most intelligent that survive from the ancient world. What is more, his interest in the history of thought led him to include the history of 'physical studies' (*phusiologia*), the history of mathematics, the history of astronomy and the history of theology, in a programme of systematic researches which he assigned his pupils. Their work in these fields was never adequately revised later, much less repeated, so that their books remained standard works of reference throughout antiquity. The history of 'physical studies' was the work of Theophrastus; those of mathematics, astronomy and theology were by Eudemus.

Theophrastus, though he accepted the Aristotelian framework, was no mindless drudge. He read the Presocratics carefully, and on particular points of interpretation he was willing to disagree with Aristotle. There is nothing to suggest that he was either dishonest or careless in his handling of the evidence. His book 'On Physical Opinions' is lost, all but a long fragment dealing with views about sensation and sense-perception, and a few small fragments quoted by Simplicius. But the greater part of what is stated in the later 'doxographic' writers about the Presocratics is simply copied directly or indirectly from this book.

Eudemus' work is also mostly lost, and also influenced the 'doxographers'. It is a pity that he was a far less reliable historian than Theophrastus, capable of wild anachronism in his interpretations, as may be demonstrated in the case of mathematics and astronomy, and suspected in the case of theology.

Later philosophers remained interested, in different ways, in the Presocratics. The Stoics aimed to show that some previous philosophers had held opinions consonant with their own, and revered Heraclitus in particular as a forerunner of Stoicism. Much confusion has been caused by Stoic interpretations of Heraclitus and others; yet it was the wide influence of the Stoics that explains the large number of genuine fragments of Heraclitus that survive. The Epicureans seem to have treated the Presocratics only as possible sources of opposition to Epicureanism, against which it was necessary to be armed; if they influenced the tradition, it was by distorting it. To certain thinkers of a sceptical turn is owed the preservation of some knowledge about the Sophists. The Neo-Platonists, finally, devised new and at least partly misleading interpretations of Heraclitus, Parmenides and Empedocles. In all the period between Theophrastus, at the end of the fourth century

B.C., to Simplicius, at the beginning of the sixth century A.D., there is very little indeed in the way of a disinterested, historical approach to the Presocratics. Simplicius at least recognised the importance of going back to the original works and quoting the original words. His indispensable contributions to our knowledge of Parmenides above all have already been described.

In the centuries following Simplicius, the original works of the Presocratics were irretrievably lost, if they had not been lost already. From now on, it was possible to study thinkers earlier than Plato only through the medium of such classical authors as survived. Apart from the works already mentioned, the most considerable sources of knowledge are other authors who quote the words of Presocratic thinkers on occasion: notably Plutarch, and one or two of the more learned of the Christian Fathers, such as Clement and Hippolytus. Wholesale forgery of Presocratic texts never occurred (except possibly in the case of the 'Pythagorean' Philolaus), so that doubts about authenticity of fragments are not frequent. But there remain, in dealing with fragments quoted by later authors, problems of text (short quotations were generally made from memory, which is inaccurate) and above all the problems of interpretation without a context.

The origins of modern study of the Presocratics were in the Germany of the romantic period, when not merely had classical studies generally reached a certain maturity, but the philosophical ferment of the time was added to a new sensitivity of historical understanding. In particular, Hegel, whose ideas for some time dominated the world of thought, explicitly directed the student of metaphysics to the study of the history of philosophy, as no philosopher since Aristotle had done. According to Hegel, it was only or principally through its development in the history of thought that 'the Spirit' (*der Geist*) manifested itself, and since 'the Spirit' was the concern of philosophy, so was the history of philosophy.

No history of the study of the Presocratics will be attempted

here. Its origins have been mentioned only in order to suggest the
kind of balance that has to be attempted in the interpretation of
the evidence. Without an accurate knowledge of the ancient Greek
language and culture, the evidence cannot be interpreted at all,
nor the thinkers placed in any historical setting. Without historical sensitivity, the interpreter will be at the mercy of his sources,
or of his own prejudices, or both. And without some philosophical
impetus, he will not be able to create a lifelike account of what his
protagonists were about, why they inquired and reasoned as they
did; at best, he will produce a hodge-podge of unrelated insights.

The previous chapters of this book have aimed at introducing
the reader to the Presocratics and at suggesting reasons why this
very specialised subject of study does and should appeal to anyone
with any general curiosity about man and the universe. It is to
philosophers and scientists, whether professional or amateur, that
the Presocratics speak, though they themselves are, in the strict
sense, neither philosophers nor scientists, but by their efforts
brought about the birth of both philosophy and science from less
formal ways of thinking. The sixth-century Ionians, stimulated
from outside by contact with older civilisations, and from within
by political and social innovation, created the grandiose vision of
a universe ruled by a divine law, omnipotent, omnipresent,
eternal and impartial; and they did their best to relate this vision
to the world as they saw it. From this attempt, paths lead in two
different directions. One path, which has been given the more
emphatic treatment in this book, leads, through the efforts of
Anaximenes and Heraclitus to make the unity of the universe a
more than merely formal one, to the consciousness of proto-
philosophical problems about unity and diversity, sameness and
opposition, and from there to the 'Copernican revolution' of
Parmenides. The other path leads to a concentration of attention
on the structures of particular things, and the attempt to explain
these structures completely in terms of certain 'key' ideas:
numbers, shapes, proportions, *krasis*, or such analogies as those
between plant and animal, or animal and *kosmos*. This second path

is that of the physiologists and cosmologists of Great Greece in the early fifth century, and is associated, rather doubtfully, with Pythagoras and his sect. To this extent, at least, the Hellenistic classification of the Presocratics into 'Eastern' and 'Western', 'Ionian' and 'Italian' schools is justified: there *is* a permanent tension, running through the whole subsequent history of science, between the universal and the particularising aspects, between global laws and local explanations.

The later fifth century, not surprisingly in view of the rapidity of the preceding developments, was the scene of considerable confusion. Those who still took cosmology seriously had to try to reconcile the Milesian scheme of things with the divergent tendencies of the two paths just mentioned. Here, Anaxagoras and the Atomists produced answers of the two different kinds possible to the problem of the structure of matter—the 'continuous' and the 'discrete' solution, respectively. Their ideas were to find no true development for over two thousand years. Those who confined themselves, at this time, to philosophical puzzles or the study of human nature were more immediately important, for, though their achievement in itself is less impressive, they created in sum a fruitful chaos which was a necessary precondition for the work of Plato and Aristotle.

Notes

The standard collection of ancient texts relating to the Presocratics is: H. Diels, *Die Fragmente der Vorsokratiker* (Berlin, 1st edn. 1903; 5th and subsequent edns., ed. by W. Kranz, 1934–7, 1951–2 &c.). In its later editions —the last to make material revisions is the sixth (1951–2)—this book is usually referred to as 'Diels-Kranz' or 'DK'. Different editions may be distinguished, if necessary, by an index number, thus: 'DK⁷'.

In Diels-Kranz, the individual thinkers, arranged in roughly chronological order, are each assigned a number. The texts relating to each are divided into A-texts, which are biographical notices and accounts by others of the man's thought, and B-texts, which are the surviving fragments of his works. (There is sometimes also a section C containing dubious and spurious fragments, and other texts of doubtful relevance.) The standard method of citing a text from Diels-Kranz is in the form 'DK 22 B 39', where the first number indicates the man, the second is the number of the B-text.

In using Diels-Kranz, it should be remembered (*a*) that in judging whether or not a certain text is or is not a genuine fragment, they are not necessarily infallible; (*b*) that the collection of A-texts is not and was never intended to be a complete collection of all relevant material.

A German translation of all the B-texts is given at the foot of the page in Diels-Kranz. There is an English translation of them by K. Freeman, *Ancilla to the Presocratic Philosophers* (Oxford, 1948), but this is unreliable. Most of the more important fragments, and many of the A-texts, are given in English translation in the standard works of Burnet, Guthrie, and Kirk-Raven (see below). For translations of texts relating to individual philosophers, see the notes to particular chapters.

In this book, fragments of the Presocratics are always cited by their B-number in Diels-Kranz, with the prefix 'fr.' Other ancient texts are cited either directly from their author, using whatever is the standard system of reference for the author in question, or occasionally from the A-texts of Diels-Kranz. The Diels-Kranz references are to any postwar edition. The text translated is not always that of Diels-Kranz.

Standard books treating the Presocratics generally:

J. Burnet, *Early Greek Philosophy* (4th edn., London 1930); lucid and stimulating, though now outdated at many points.

W. K. C. Guthrie, *A History of Greek Philosophy* Vols. I, II and III (Cambridge, 1962, 1965, 1969); very full and sensible though not incisive. Best for consultation on particular points of detail.

G. S. Kirk and J. E. Raven, *The Presocratic Philosophers* (Cambridge 1957; subsequently issued in paperback); uneven in quality. At its best informative and cautious.

E. Zeller, *Die Philosophie der Griechen in ihrer geschichtlichen Entwicklung,* Erster Teil (6th edn., ed. by W. Nestle, Leipzig 1919–20); extremely thorough and detailed; the most useful of the older works.

The following are generally relevant and of value:

E. R. Dodds, *The Greeks and the Irrational* (Berkeley and Los Angeles, 1951);

S. Sambursky, *The Physical World of the Greeks* (London, 1956); (both of these have appeared in paperback).

B. Snell, *The Discovery of the Mind,* [translated from the German by T. G. Rosenmeyer] (Oxford, 1953);

H. Lloyd-Jones, *The Justice of Zeus* (Berkeley, Los Angeles and London, 1971).

A collection of recent shorter papers, mostly more specialised:

D. J. Furley and R. E. Allen (editors), *Studies in Presocratic Philosophy,* Vol. I (London, 1970), Vol. II (to appear shortly).

*

In the notes to chapters, which follow, the books referred to are, as far as is possible, recent books in English. References to papers in specialist journals, and to books in languages other than English, have been made only when these are particularly valuable.

Books mentioned in the introductory section above are referred to in the notes to chapters by authors' or editors' names only.

CHAPTER ONE

(1) Original texts in translation:

(*i*) Early Greek Literature.

There are many translations of Homer. The remains of the early lyric and elegiac poets are translated (though not very reliably) in the Loeb series of translations by J. M. Edmonds (*Lyra Graeca* I–III; *Greek Elegy and Iambus* I–II); Hesiod in the same series by H. G. Evelyn-White.

(*ii*) Ancient Near Eastern texts.

A wide selection in *Ancient Near Eastern Texts relating to the Old Testament*, ed. J. B. Pritchard (3rd edn., Princeton, 1969). The Old Testament itself, particularly Job and the prophets, throws much light on the thought-world of the Ancient Near East.

(*iii*) Iranian and Hindu texts.

The Hymns of Zarathustra, trans. J. Duchesne-Guillemin (trans. from the French by M. Henning) (London, 1952).

Hindu Scriptures, selected translated and introduced by R. C. Zaehner (London, 1966).

Inscriptions of Darius in: R. G. Kent, *Old Persian* (2nd edn. New Haven, 1953).

(2) Books for reference and further reading:

A general reference work: *The Cambridge Ancient History*, ed. J. B. Bury, S. A. Cook and F. E. Adcock, Vols. I to IV (Cambridge, 1923–6). The first two volumes are now in many ways outdated, and are being replaced, in the so-called 'Third Edition', by two entirely new volumes. Of these, at the time of writing, Vol. I, Parts 1 and 2 ed. I. E. S. Edwards, C. J. Gadd, and N. G. L. Hammond, has appeared (Cambridge, 1970 and 1971); and many chapters of Vol. II have been published separately.

A selection of other books on subjects touched on in this chapter.*

(*i*) Aspects of Greek civilisation from the tenth to sixth centuries:

J. B. Bury, *A History of Greece* (3rd. edn., revised by R. Meiggs, London 1959);

A. Andrewes, *The Greeks* (London, 1967);

A. Andrewes, *The Greek Tyrants* (London, 1956);

A. R. Burn, *The Lyric Age of Greece* (London, 1960);

A. Zimmern, *The Greek Commonwealth* (5th edn., Oxford, 1931);

J. M. Cook, *The Greeks in Ionia and the East* (London, 1962);

T. J. Dunbabin, *The Greeks and their Eastern Neighbours* (London, 1957);

J. Boardman, *The Greeks Overseas* (London, 1964);

* Many of these have been published in paperback editions.

J. Boardman, *Greek Art* (London, 1964);

G. S. Kirk, *The Songs of Homer* (Cambridge, 1962);

C. M. Bowra, *Greek Lyric Poetry* (2nd edn., Oxford, 1961).

(*ii*) Aspects of Ancient Near Eastern and Iranian civilisation:

H. R. Hall, *The Ancient History of the Near East* (9th edn., London, 1936);

A. H. Gardiner, *Egypt of the Pharaohs* (Oxford, 1961);

O. Neugebauer, *The Exact Sciences in Antiquity* (2nd edn., Providence, 1957);

H. Frankfort and others, *Before Philosophy* (London, 1949);

R. C. Zaehner, *The Dawn and Twilight of Zoroastrianism* (London, 1961);

D. Harden, *The Phoenicians* (London, 1962).

(*iii*) Other topics:

D. Diringer, *Writing* (London, 1962);

J. Goody (editor), *Literacy in Traditional Societies* (Cambridge, 1968);

Sir J. Hicks, *A Theory of Economic History* (Oxford, 1969);

M. Bloch, *Feudal Society* (2 vols. trans. L. A. Manyon, London, 1961–2).

CHAPTER TWO

Hesiod's *Theogony* has been edited recently with valuable Prolegomena and Commentary by M. L. West (Oxford, 1966). On Xenophanes, his theology, and that of other early Presocratics: W. Jaeger, *The Theology of the Early Greek Philosophers* (Oxford, 1947). On Iranian religion and Zoroaster, see notes to Chapter One; also J. Duchesne-Guillemin, *La Religion de L'Iran Ancienne* (Paris, 1962). For Hebrew religious thought of this period, the book of Job and those of the earlier prophets are instructive.

On the Milesians, besides the books mentioned in the introduction to Notes above, see C. H. Kahn, *Anaximander and the Origins of Greek Cosmology* (New York, 1960).

The whole question of Near Eastern influence is treated in: M. L. West *Early Greek Philosophy and the Orient* (Oxford, 1971). This work contains many useful assemblages of evidence; it is ingenious, and sometimes convincing, in its reconstructions, but it exaggerates the importance of Near Eastern influences for the Presocratics. For the Phoenician cosmogonies, see references in this book.

Early Greek astronomy: D. R. Dicks, *Early Greek Astronomy to Aristotle* (London, 1970), good but too dogmatic on the early Presocratics; see C. H. Kahn, 'On Early Greek Astronomy', in *Journal of Hellenic Studies* 90 (1970), 99–116.

Early Greek mathematics: there is no good account, owing to almost total lack of good evidence (the standard history of Greek mathematics, by Sir T. L. Heath, is not sufficiently critical for the period before 400). Some suggestive remarks in Neugebauer (see notes to Chapter One).

On Pherecydes and Alcman: M. L. West, *Early Greek Philosophy and the Orient* (see above), chs. 1 and 2; the same author in *Classical Quarterly*, 57 (1963), 154–76.

CHAPTER THREE

The fragments of Heraclitus, as those of all Presocratics, are cited in this book from Diels-Kranz. There is a new edition (with commentary and English translation) of the fragments, with different numbering, by M. Marcovich (Merida, Venezuela, 1967). This is valuable for its collection of paraphrases and Heraclitean allusions in later authors, which sometimes help to determine the text and meaning of a fragment. The edition of Bywater (Oxford, 1877), though now superseded, is also serviceable in this respect.

The indispensable work of G. S. Kirk, *Heraclitus: the Cosmic Fragments* (Cambridge, 1954; reprinted with some substantial corrections, 1962) provides an elaborate commentary on most of the more important fragments. Besides the books mentioned in the introduction to Notes above, see also H. Fränkel, 'A Thought Pattern in Heraclitus', in *American Journal of Philology*, 59 (1938), 309–37.

To Wittgenstein, the best introduction is the *Tractatus Logico-Philosophicus* itself, in the translation of D. F. Pears and B. F. McGuinness (London, 1961). See also D. F. Pears, *Wittgenstein* (London, 1971).

Heraclitus and Oriental influences: much interesting material in M. L. West, *Early Greek Philosophy and the Orient* (see above) ch. 6, who rightly insists that the question of Oriental influences in Heraclitus deserves more serious consideration than it has generally received before now. Nevertheless, it seems at present unlikely that such influences were decisively important, or that they can help us to understand better the central concerns of Heraclitus' thought.

For Diogenes Laertius, see Notes to Chapter Eight. On *harmoniē* in Greek music: I. Henderson, 'Ancient Greek Music', in *The New Oxford History of Music*, Vol. I. *Ancient and Oriental Music*, ed. E. Wellesz (London, 1957). On Greek bows: A. M. Snodgrass, *Arms and Armour of the Greeks* (London, 1967).

CHAPTER FOUR

On the Greek West at this time: J. Boardman, *The Greeks Overseas* (see Notes to Chapter One); T. J. Dunbabin, *The Western Greeks* (Oxford, 1948); M. I. Finley, *Ancient Sicily* (London, 1968).

Pythagoras: the best study of the sources is W. Burkert, *Weisheit and Wissenschaft* (Nuremberg, 1962); a clear but less critical account in Guthrie, Vol. I. Greek texts containing Pythagorean *akousmata* are printed in Diels-

Kranz 58c. On shamanism and related topics, see Dodds, especially ch. 5. On mathematics, astronomy and music see the references in the notes to Chapters One, Two and Three. On the Chinese Taoists: J. Needham, *Science and Civilisation in China*, Vol. II (Cambridge, 1969), ch. 10.

Empedocles: for his cosmology see Chapter Seven. The relations between his cosmology and his religious beliefs are still a subject of controversy. The following treatments should be mentioned: Guthrie, Vol. II, ch. 3; C. H. Kahn, 'Religion and Natural Philosophy in Empedocles' Doctrine of the Soul', in *Archiv für Geschichte der Philosophie*, 42 (1960), 3–35; and J. Bollack, *Empédocle* (Paris, 1965–9); also G. Zuntz, *Persephone* (Oxford, 1971).

Early medicine and physiology: no satisfactory special treatment. See Guthrie, chapters on Alcmaeon (Vol. I), Parmenides and Empedocles (Vol. II). On sense-perception: the books of Beare and Stratton (see notes to Chapter Six).

CHAPTER FIVE

A recent edition of Parmenides, L. Tarán, *Parmenides, a Text with Translation, Commentary and Critical Essays* (Princeton, 1965), is unsatisfactory, but informative about modern scholarly opinion. The best introduction to the main problems remains G. E. L. Owen, 'Eleatic Questions', in *Classical Quarterly*, 54 (1960), 84–102 (to be reprinted in *Studies in Presocratic Philosophy*, Vol. II (see introduction to Notes above)). A. P. D. Mourelatos, *The Route of Parmenides* (New Haven and London, 1970) contains much interesting material, though its treatment of the arguments is unconvincing.

On the proem: C. M. Bowra, 'The Proem of Parmenides', in *Classical Philology*, 32 (1937), 97–112, reprinted in the author's *Problems in Greek Poetry* (Oxford, 1953); W. Burkert, 'Das Proömium des Parmenides und die Katabasis des Pythagoras' in *Phronesis*, 14 (1969), 1–30.

Zeno: a translation of the fragments in *Zeno of Elea, a Text with Translation and Notes*, by H. D. P. Lee (Cambridge, 1936). On the various arguments, see H. Fränkel, 'Zeno of Elea's Attacks on Plurality', in *American Journal of Philology*, 63 (1942), 1–25, 193–206; G. E. L. Owen, 'Zeno and the Mathematicians', in *Proceedings of the Aristotelian Society*, 58 (1957–8), 199–222; G. Vlastos, 'A Note on Zeno's Arrow', in *Phronesis*, 11 (1966), 3–18, and 'Zeno's Race Course', in *Journal of the History of Philosophy*, 4 (1966) 95–108; and the commentary of W. D. Ross on Aristotle, *Physics*, Book VI in his edition of the *Physics* (Oxford, 1936).

Recent philosophical discussion of Zeno has been copious. On the relation of the paradoxes to modern problems in the philosophy of science, see for instance A. Grünbaum, *Modern Science and Zeno's Paradoxes* (London, 1968).

Texts in translation: the medical writings of this period from the 'Hippocratic corpus' are translated into English in the Loeb volumes, *Hippocrates* I–IV, ed. W. H. S. Jones. The most rewarding, for those without a medical training, are: 'On Ancient Medicine', 'Airs Waters Places', 'Epidemics I and III' (all Vol. I); 'On the Sacred Disease' (Vol. II). Thucydides: various translations, e.g. in the Penguin series by R. Warner. The early Platonic dialogues, especially *Protagoras, Gorgias* and *Republic*, Book I, give a brilliant though partisan view of sophists and their ideas, as well as of Socrates; these dialogues, as well as Plato's *Apology* and Xenophon's *Memorabilia* (for Socrates), are translated in the Penguin series. The *Protagoras* in English translation with a good introduction by G. Vlastos in the Library of Liberal Arts series (1956). The remains of the sophists themselves, including Cratylus, Lycophron and the *Dissoi Logoi*, in Diels-Kranz Vol. II.

The sophistic period generally: Guthrie, Vol. III. Particular sophists: on Protagoras, see the introduction by G. Vlastos mentioned above; on Gorgias, introduction by E. R. Dodds to his edition of the *Gorgias* (Oxford, 1959). On Socrates, G. Vlastos (ed.), *The Philosophy of Socrates* (New York, 1971). On Thucydides: J. H. Finley, *Thucydides* (Harvard, 1942).

Problems of sense-perception: J. I. Beare, *Greek Theories of Elementary Cognition* (Oxford, 1906); G. M. Stratton (see notes to Chapter Eight); C. Bailey (see notes to Chapter Seven).

Morals, politics, the nature and history of human society: E. A. Havelock, *The Liberal Temper in Greek Politics* (London, 1957) is stimulating but uneven, and speculative sometimes to the point of fantasy. A. W. H. Adkins, *Merit and Responsibility* (Oxford, 1960) has much of interest but is blinkered by conceptual rigidity. Dodds, ch. 6, Lloyd-Jones, ch. 6.

Parmenides' cosmology: J. S. Morrison, 'Parmenides and Er', in *Journal of Hellenic Studies*, 75 (1955), 59–68.

Empedocles' system has been much debated recently. See the references in the Notes to Chapter Four, and: D. O'Brien, *Empedocles' Cosmic Cycle* (Cambridge, 1969); F. Solmsen, 'Love and Strife in Empedocles' cosmology', in *Phronesis*, 10 (1965), 109–48. The *peri hebdomadōn*: M. L. West, in *Classical Quarterly*, 65 (1971), 365–88.

The 'Pythagoreans' of the late fifth century: Guthrie, Vol. I, ch. 4.

Anaxagoras: G. Vlastos in *Philosophical Review*, 59 (1950), 31–57; C. Strang in *Archiv für Geschichte der Philosophie*, 45 (1963), 101–18, in addition to the accounts in Kirk-Raven and Guthrie, who may also be consulted for the

minor late Presocratics not discussed in this chapter. The views about Anaxagoras expressed in this chapter owe something to conversations with Mr. M.
Schofield.

The Atomists: C. Bailey, *The Greek Atomists and Epicurus* (Oxford, 1928);
V. E. Alfieri, *Atomos Idea* (Florence, 1953).

CHAPTER EIGHT

The works of Aristotle are translated into English in the Oxford Translation
of Aristotle (12 vols., Oxford, 1908–1952); for the biological works, the
translations with valuable notes by A. L. Peck in the Loeb series are preferable.
The Greek texts and commentaries of W. D. Ross (Oxford, various dates
between 1924 and 1961) are indispensable for more detailed study.

The surviving long fragment of Theophrastus 'On Physical Opinions' is
edited with English translation, notes and introductory essay by G. M.
Stratton, *Theophrastus and the Greek Physiological Psychology before Aristotle*
(London, 1917; reprinted Amsterdam, 1964).

The 'Lives of the Philosophers' by Diogenes Laertius, available in the Loeb
series, is a scissors-and-paste compilation which, however, sometimes (e.g. on
Heraclitus) gives the fullest version of the doxographical tradition descending
from Theophrastus.

On the interrelations of the doxographic writers, the fundamental work is
H. Diels, *Doxographi Graeci* (Berlin, 1879; reprinted 1929 and later) (in
Latin). A summary of Diels' conclusions in Burnet (pp. 33–7), and in Kirk-
Raven (pp. 3–6).

On the important question of the merits and limitations of Aristotle and
Theophrastus as historians of philosophy: H. Cherniss, *Aristotle's Criticism
of Presocratic Philosophy* (Baltimore, 1935; reprinted New York, 1964); J. B.
McDiarmid, 'Theophrastus and the Presocratic Causes', in *Harvard Studies in
Classical Philology*, 61 (1953), 85–156 (both of these important but one-sided
studies); C. H. Kahn, *Anaximander* &c. (see notes to Chapter Two), pp. 17–
24; W. K. C. Guthrie, 'Aristotle as a Historian of Philosophy', in *Journal of
Hellenic Studies*, 77 (1957), 35–41.

A recent controversy about the relation of the Presocratics to science:
K. R. Popper, 'Back to the Presocratics', in *Proceedings of the Aristotelian
Society*, 59 (1958–9), 1–24 (reprinted, with revisions, in the author's *Conjectures
and Refutations* (London, 3rd edn. 1969) and in Furley-Allen); G. S. Kirk in
Mind, 69 (1960), 318–39 (also in Furley-Allen); K. R. Popper in *Mind*, 72
(1963), 386–92 (more fully in *Conjectures and Refutations*); G. E. R. Lloyd in
British Journal for the Philosophy of Science, 18 (1967), 21–38.

Index